COMMISSION OF THE EUROPEAN COMMUNITIES

Jean GROUX

Conseiller d'État

Honorary Director-General,
Commission of the European
Communities

Philippe MANIN

Professor, University of Paris I
(Panthéon-Sorbonne)

Director of the Centre universitaire
d'études des Communautés européennes

The European Communities in the international order

Preface by President Gaston E. THORN

THE EUROPEAN PERSPECTIVES SERIES
BRUSSELS

This publication was prepared outside the Commission of the European Communities and is intended as a contribution to public debate on the European Communities in the international order. It does not necessarily reflect the opinion of the Commission.

This publication is also available in

DA   ISBN 92-825-5180-6
DE   ISBN 92-825-4288-2
GR   ISBN 92-825-5181-4
FR   ISBN 92-825-4356-0
IT   ISBN 92-825-5182-2
NL   ISBN 92-825-4756-6
ES   ISBN 92-825-5183-0
PT   ISBN 92-825-4757-4

Cataloguing data appear at the end of this publication

Luxembourg: Office for Official Publications of the European Communities, 1985

ISBN 92-825-5137-7

Catalogue number: CB-40-84-206-EN-C

Preface

The Treaties of Paris and Rome started the Six, and later the Nine and the Ten, on the road towards a union which was bound to affect their relations with the rest of the world and could not develop in an orderly manner without the conduct of some of those relations being transferred to the Community.

Such a change was only possible on two conditions: firstly, the Community must have the assurance, with the willing agreement of the Member States, that it could at all times speak 'with one voice' in dealings with non-member countries and, secondly, those countries must be willing 'to recognize' the Community and to negotiate with it.

The very large number of agreements to which the Community is party with developed and developing countries in all parts of the world and the fact that many of them are of the widest economic and political scope bear witness to the reality of the change and to the importance which the Community has taken on as a new actor on the international stage.

It has to be added that, while the Community has no powers in some major areas of foreign policy, this is partly offset by the practice of collective action by Member States, in particular through political cooperation and by the frequent combination of this practice with international activities within the field of competence of the Community (negotiations, dialogues and 'mixed' agreements with non-member countries and the adoption of a concerted position by the Community and its Member States in international organizations and at international conferences).

However, the affirmation of a 'European identity in dealings with the rest of the world' as embodied in the Copenhagen Declaration of 1973 and reiterated in subsequent decisions of Heads of State or Government of the Member States sometimes comes up against obstacles both within and outside the Community.

Firstly, in some areas where the Community is in fact empowered to act by the Treaties, Member States continue to handle individually all or part of their relations with third countries.

Secondly and most important, Member States' difficulty in agreeing even on questions for which they accept that joint action is an obligation or a necessity, has often prevented the Community from presenting a united front in international negotiations or from having greater influence on their outcome.

3

The attitudes of non-member countries to Europe naturally differ.

The USSR and its allies are alone in maintaining a negative attitude on principle, expressed by their refusal to recognize the Community in any way.

By contrast, the Western countries have always given their political support to the building of Europe, even if, in defence of their own interests, they frequently criticize particular aspects of Community policies.

The attitude of other non-member countries to the Community is generally positive or at least open, but some of them do not understand clearly how it works and they sometimes have difficulty in understanding that it wishes to establish an international personality separate from that of its Member States.

This factor, combined with the opposition of the East European countries has often worked against participation by the Community in the work of certain international organizations or conferences and in the multilateral instruments or agreements worked out on such occasions.

This is, in a way, the background to the study by Mr Jean Groux and Mr Philippe Manin on 'The European Communities in the international order' published under the auspices of the Commission.

It will fill a gap.

There are already many studies on the international powers and activities of the Community but almost all are concerned exclusively with how those powers and activities are related to the 'internal order' of the organization.

This study approaches the problem from the outside, from the standpoint of international law.

From that standpoint, it discusses many questions which have been solved – and remain to be solved – by negotiation with non-member countries, in order to fit the Community into the rules and machinery of an international order which was framed by and for States and is ill-suited technically and politically to admit other entities, and particularly the Community which differs clearly from traditional international organizations.

This study by Mr Groux and Mr Manin which is the product of a great deal of work and experience should, therefore, meet the needs of everyone, whether or not members of the legal profession, who wishes to have an in-depth account of and detailed information on this complex subject.

Gaston E. THORN

Contents

PART TWO : PARTICIPATION OF THE EUROPEAN COMMUNITIES IN INTERNATIONAL AGREEMENTS AND OTHER LEGAL INSTRUMENTS 55

Introduction

The problem of the European Communities' place in the international legal order is becoming increasingly more important as the scale of their activities in the field of international relations increases.[1]

In practice, international law normally recognizes only limited legal capacity in any subject of international law which is not a State.

Setting aside a number of special marginal categories, this applies first and foremost to intergovernmental international organizations which are structures created by the decision of States by international treaty.

Admittedly, the international capacity of international organizations is now remarkably wide as compared with the rules which prevailed at the start of the twentieth century or even during the inter-war period.

For example, the right is no longer disputed for an organization to conclude a treaty necessary for the performance of its duties, with one or more States or with other international organizations.

It is also accepted that an organization can lodge an international claim, that is to say it can sue another subject of international law for damages (and conversely can be sued).[2]

It is also established that organizations enjoy privileges and immunities which put them in much the same position as States in that respect.

However, in spite of their role in international life, no-one claims that international organizations currently have a legal status equal to that of a State.

---

[1] The three European Communities, the European Coal and Steel Community (ECSC), the European Economic Community (EEC) and the European Atomic Energy Community (EAEC or Euratom) were established by separate treaties, but have been organically united since their institutions were 'merged' in 1967. In this study, the term 'Communities' refers to all three. In the case of foreign relations in particular, the legal foundations contained in the respective Treaties are not, in fact, the same for the three Communities. Where the question is of sufficient importance, reference is made to the individual features of the ECSC and the EAEC. Obviously, however, this analysis, which is applicable to all three 'Communities' is concerned mainly with the EEC.

[2] Cf. the opinion given by the International Court of Justice on 11.4.1949, concerning compensation for damage suffered in the service of the United Nations (ICJ, 1949, p. 174).

This is demonstrated by numerous examples.

Thus, in the field of diplomatic relations, international organizations do not have the right to set up fully-fledged legations, but similar bodies of lesser rank.

In the matter of contractual relations, it is still not generally accepted that an international organization may take part, except as an observer, in major diplomatic conferences held to draft the general multilateral treaties which today constitute a kind of international legislation.

International organizations can often participate in the actual treaties only by way of procedures which distinguish them as not ranking as States. For example, international organizations with competence for space activities cannot be full parties to the Space Treaty of 27 January 1967 but can only deposit a declaration stating that they will be bound by the rights and obligations embodied in that treaty.

In the matter of relations between institutions, an international organization can rarely itself become a full member of another organization. In most cases, it has to be content with observer status.

Finally, as regards the peaceful settlement of disputes, international organizations cannot bring a case before the International Court of Justice under the terms of the Court's statute.

It can very reasonably be accepted as normal that international organizations should have only limited capacity because they derive, after all, from the will of the States concerned.

Nevertheless, status as defined by international custom can prove rigid or inappropriate when applied to a grouping such as the Communities.

It could, of course, be argued that the Communities do not come within this category because of their special nature. Some supporters of this view have emphasized the word 'Community' and the fact that it is a grouping of peoples as well as a grouping of States.

However, the Communities were set up by international treaty between States and vested with their own institutions, and are clearly *ipso facto* international organizations.

Moreover, there seems to be no doubt that they are prepared to see themselves as such. For example, it is as such that they have several times submitted comments to the Secretary-General of the United Nations on texts drafted by the International Law Commission (ILC) when that body decided to ask international organizations to comment on its drafts.[1]

---

[1] Under ILC practice, the organizations concerned are the UN and intergovernmental organizations which are invited to send observers to UN codifying conferences.

It is also as international organizations that they have observer status with organizations and at conferences within the United Nations system.

Furthermore, the legal category of international organization is broad enough to include a very wide variety of institutions.

In other words, the inclusion of the Communities in this category in no way limits their specific character or the problems they may raise in the context of international relations.

Such problems stem, firstly, from the basic principles underlying the Communities and, secondly, from the complexity of the Community system.

The fundamental principle of this system is that, within the area specifed by the Treaties, the Communities exercise powers for and in place of the Member States.

The EEC Treaty (Article 113) provided for the application of this principle to commercial relations. The EEC had powers from the outset to conclude commercial agreements and became solely competent to do so on the expiry of the transitional period (1 January 1970).[1]

This single area would have been enough to establish the importance of the Communities' international powers.

The organization's practice has gone much further, however. Through a whole series of rulings, the Court of Justice of the European Communities has considerably widened the scope of these international powers, by laying down the principle that each internal legal power is at least potentially matched by an international legal power. Of course, as long as this competence is not effectively exercised, other than in cases of exclusive powers, the States retain the right to enter individually into international commitments, provided that they do not limit the Communities' contractual autonomy. But, as soon as the Communities have used an international power, the Member States in principle lose that power.[2]

---

[1] Regarding the nature and extent of the EEC's powers in respect of commercial policy, see in particular ECR Opinion 1/75 of 14.7.1975, 1975 ECR 1355; Opinion 1/78 of 4.10.1979, 1979 ECR 2871; C.D. Ehlermann, 'The scope of Article 113 of the EEC Treaty' in Mélanges en l'honneur de P.H.Teitgen, Pedone, Paris, 1984, pp. 145-169.

[2] The essential steps in the case-law of the Court of Justice are: Judgment of 31.3.1971, Case 22/70, AETR 1971 ECR 263; Judgment of 14.7.1976, Joined Cases 3, 4 and 6/67 Kramer 1976 ECR 1279; Opinion 1/76 of 26.4.1977, 1977 ECR 741. See in particular, A. Georgiadou, Quelques problèmes juridiques posés en droit international public et en droit communautaire et l'arrêt AETR de la CJCE, Thesis, Paris 11, 1974; W.J. Ganshof van der Meersch, Les relations extérieures de la CEE dans le domaine des politiques communes et l'arrêt de la Cour de justice du 31.3.1971, Cahiers de Droit européen (CDE) 1972, pp. 127-158; J. Groux, Le parallélisme des compétences internes et externes de la CEE, CDE, 1978, pp. 3-32; R. Kovar, La contribution de la Cour de justice au développement de la condition internationale de la Communauté européenne, CDE 1978, p. 527 et seq.

In other words, far from being limited once and for all to commercial agreements and association agreements with non-member countries, transfers of international powers can be extended to other areas, as already shown by the international agreements concluded by the EEC on such subjects as transport, agriculture, fisheries and the protection of the environment.

In all areas of exclusive Community competence, third parties must henceforth deal with Community institutions only. Similarly, when multilateral negotiations take place, the Communities must take part for, and in place of, the Member States.

The non-member countries concerned must of course be willing to accept the substitution.

Already concerned by the fact that they have to deal not with States but with an international organization, third parties also have to put up with the inherent complexity of the Community system, for which there are several reasons.

Firstly, the fields in which the Communities have the sole right to deal with non-member States at any given time are not clear from the Treaties establishing the respective Communities. Account has to be taken of the principles laid down in the rulings of the Court, particularly as to whether the Communities' powers have already been used.

Secondly, the extent of their international powers is bound to vary in the course of time.

From the outset, such changes were built in by the establishment of the transitional periods provided for in the Community Treaties. They also stem from the aforementioned conditions for the use of Community powers. Lastly, they spring from the fact that the Communities can add new policies to those listed in the Treaties, in particular by making use of Article 235 of the EEC Treaty.

In view of these facts, it is understandable that non-member countries feel occasionally obliged to ask the Communities and the Member States for a list of the Community powers, as happened in the case of the Convention on the Law of the Sea.

It is equally understandable that the Communities are unwilling to accede to this demand precisely because their powers are not clearly defined.

Thirdly, as it is impossible in many cases to match the subject of international negotiations exactly to either the area of Community competence or the area of State powers, the practice of the 'mixed' agreement has been devised, associating the Community and its Member States as a kind of complex party. There is no clear way of determining the cases which require a mixed agreement and the matter is often a source of disagreement between the Commission and Member States, which in fact try to maximize the area covered by mixed agreements. Any systematic application is therefore difficult and non-member countries may therefore be surprised to be faced sometimes by the Community alone and sometimes by the Community and its Member States.

Fourthly, there are a number of activities linked with the common market, in respect of which the Treaty conferred on the Community institutions only powers to coordinate the Member States' activities. The Member States therefore continue to take a direct part in international negotiations but within the context and limits of concerted action.

For example, under Article 116 of the EEC Treaty, the Member States are required to proceed by common action within the framework of international organizations of an economic character on 'matters of particular interest to the common market'. Under the same article, the Commission and the Council are required to work out the terms of such common action.[1]

Furthermore, practice in this area has added to the cases covered by the Treaty. While the Communities have, for the time being, foregone the exercise of some or all of the powers vested in them, at least potentially, by the Treaties, they have subjected Member States' action to prior or subsequent Community monitoring.

For example, a number of provisions require Council or Commission approval for the adoption by Member States of certain trade policy measures (variation of import quotas, application of safeguard clauses, etc.)[2] Other examples are the numerous instruments adopted by the Council to ensure or promote ratification by all Member States of certain international conventions. The most typical example is unquestionably the Council Regulation of 15 May 1979 which required the concerted ratification by Member States of the Code of Conduct for Maritime Conferences adopted by Unctad in 1974 and formulated reservations to accompany all the ratifications.[3]

The existence of such 'Community' activities carried on by the Member States may cause difficult problems for non-member countries which may be temped to challenge not only the States which initiate such activities but also the Community which instigates them, at least when it has done more than adopt rules of procedure and has ruled on the substance of measures to be taken by the Member States.

Fifthly, the collectivity composed of the Member States is now involved in international relations, outside its own sphere of competence, through use of the machinery for political cooperation.[4] This machinery does not of course permit Member States to con-·

---

[1] Similarly, Articles 73 and 74 of the ECSC Treaty empower the Commission to make 'recommendations' to Member States (which are binding as to the aims to be pursued) for the coordination of some of their commercial policy measures (administration of import and export licences, quantitative restrictions, anti-dumping measures, etc.). Article 103 of the Euratom Treaty also imposes a restriction on the Member States through the requirement that the Commission and, where applicable, the Court of Justice must declare that there is no impediment before those States may conclude international treaties which concern the field of application of the said Treaty.

[2] On this subject, see the Council Regulations of 5.2.1982 (OJ L 35, 1982), concerning the import of products from non-member countries other than State-trading countries and China and of 30.6.1982 (OJ L 195, 1982) and 14.11.1983 (OJ L 346, 1983) concerning the import of products from State-trading countries and China.

[3] OJ L 121, 1979.

[4] On political cooperation, see: D. Hurd, 'Political Cooperation', International Affairs, Vol. 57, No 3, 1981, pp.383-393; P. Bruckner, 'La Coopération politique européenne', Revue du Marché commun, 1982, pp.59-63; E. Stein, 'European Political Cooperation (EPC) as a component of the European Foreign Affairs System', Zeitschrift für Ausländisches Öffentliches Recht und Völkerrecht, No 43, 1983, pp.49-69.

clude an international agreement collectively, but it does allow them to adopt common positions which to the outside world represent the 'Community', even though this is not really so in the legal sense of the term.

This duality is another factor which does not help to make things clear to the outside world.

Lastly, 'Community law' constitutes a complex, stratified legal system, administered by a highly-developed judicial hierarchy. Some principles of Community law may be applicable to the international rules binding the Communities. In this respect, it is true that the problems are of the same nature as for a State. Here again, however, non-member countries are unwilling to allow such questions in relation to an international organization.

Any study of the Communities' place in the international order therefore involves raising a series of issues and describing situations not normally discussed in connection with an international organization.

The crux of many of these problems is the concept of Community access to the procedures and instruments of international law.

By the very fact of its powers replacing those of the Member States, the Community, more than any other international organization, should have access to international negotiations (Part One). When the application of the theory of recognition to the Communities and their use of the prerogatives attaching to the right to establish legations have been dealt with as a kind of preliminary issue, the fundamental problem is whether and how the Communities take part in and make their voice heard in international conferences and organizations.

Although still a problem of access, it was thought best, in view of its importance, to devote a separate section to the subject of Community involvement in international treaties and other international legal instruments (Part Two).

The study of these two questions is based on already extensive practice.

By contrast, although reference is made to existing practice, Part Three deals with questions which are more a matter for the future. They are also more varied and range from the application of the Treaties to the settlement of disputes and the international liability of the Communities. They have been brought together under the title 'The European Communities and the application of international law'.

This study, which sets out essentially to examine Community action from an external viewpoint,does not go into great detail concerning the international powers of the Communities according to the principles of Community law. For example, there is no lengthy discussion of the way in which powers to conclude Treaties are distributed between the various Community institutions. This subject has already been considered in full in studies on Community institutional law. There is no need to return to it here, therefore.

Finally, the authors have in all cases preferred a neutral description of a practice to a value judgment. In many respects, the Communities are still little known despite the many studies dealing with them. The main purpose of this study is therefore to provide information.

PART ONE

Entry of the European Communities into international relations

International relations are the contacts established between the various members of international society. In order to understand the classic problems of international law, the first, almost preliminary, question is whether and how far any subject of that law (especially when that subject has special characteristics) must have been 'recognized' by the others in order to participate in international relations (Chapter I).

These international contacts are made by organs qualified to represent the subjects of international law. Some of the organs concerned are specialized; others are not. The question is where the Communities stand in relation to the practice gradually established by States (Chapter II).

The purpose of most such contacts is to start discussions or negotiations. As long as international negotiations are limited to two or a few parties and remain discreet, if not secret, there is not a great deal of formality and issues of principle rarely arise. The same is not true when the context is one of those great international 'forums' in the shape of 'conferences' or meetings of the deliberative bodies of international organizations (Chapter III).

Chapter I – The Communities and international recognition

Recognition deprives the grantor of the right to contest the existence of validity of what he has recognized. So defined, recognition, which can apply to any fact or situation, is a normal act of international life.[1]

Recognition assumes special importance when it involves accepting that some entity has qualified to rank as a given type of international law subject and is therefore entitled to claim for itself the privileges attaching to that status. This is the purpose of 'recognizing a State' or, at a lower level, a belligerent or an insurgent.[2]

The political aspect of the formal act of recognition has been emphasized on many occasions.

The fact is that the recognition of a new State assumes its greatest significance when the State in question has come into being as a result of conflict, so that a choice has to be made between one side and another (recognition of the United States during the War of Independence). The same applies to the recognition of a government, as has been seen often enough regarding the choice of Beijing (formerly Peking) or Taipeh as being entitled to represent China.

It is equally true that absence of recognition does not prevent the existence of relations between two subjects which theoretically do not recognize each other, as in the case of relations between the German Democratic Republic (East Germany) and the Federal Republic of Germany (West Germany) before the adoption of the 'Ostpolitik'.

International practice has not yet developed a theory for the 'recognition of international organizations' as it has for the 'recognition of a State'.

---

[1] J. Verhoeven, *La reconnaissance internationale dans la pratique contemporaine*, Pedone, Paris, 1979 (exhaustive bibliography).

[2] Recognition of a government means acceptance that a given organ is qualified to represent the subject it claims to represent at international level. Although theoretically different, recognition of a government often gives rise to the same questions as recognition of a State. The point at issue is whether the organ concerned, which is qualified to speak for a State, is entitled to use on its own behalf the privileges inherent in the condition of being a State.

There is no formal act of recognition of an international organization. The establishment of a mission with such an organization does not have the same significance as the establishment of diplomatic relations with a State.

All this stems from the fact that, as far as States are concerned, the creation of an international organization and its exercise of its powers are not of sufficient importance and significance for the practice applied to States to be applied to such organizations. It also stems from the fact that the essential issue for an organization is the extent of its powers, case by case, and not access to a category.

However, practice in the case of the Communities shows a number of special features.

Having first asked whether there is a practice as regards 'recognition of the European Communities' (Section 1), it now becomes necessary to ask, conversely, whether the Communities exercise the power to recognize other subjects (Section 2)?

Section 1: Recognition 'of' the European Communities

Having first noted that practices as regards recognition and, more important, non-recognition of the Communities have hitherto been comparable to that applied in the case of States (A), it next has to be asked what are the consequences of non-recognition of the Communities (B).

A – Practice as regards recognition or non-recognition of the Communities

The application of the theory of recognition to a subject of law only becomes fully apparent when other subjects adopt a formal act of recognition – or conversely of non-recognition – of that subject or establish diplomatic relations with it.

So far, the connection between recognition and the Communities is manifested mainly in the form of explicit declarations of non-recognition or the adoption of equivalent attitudes.

Such attitudes have until now been confined to the Soviet Union and the East European countries.[1]

In 1963, for example, the Soviet Minister for Foreign Trade refused to accept an EEC document handed to him by the Netherlands Ambassador to Moscow.

---

[1] Yugoslavia, which has had a mission in Brussels since 1978 does not, of course, come into this category.

The declarations made by the head of the Soviet delegation at certain international conferences attended by an EEC delegation provide an even clearer illustration. The tenor of these declarations was that participation by the USSR side by side with the EEC 'in no way signified recognition of that organization' and that 'any commitment entered into by the USSR would be with countries acting individually and not as members of the EEC'.[1]

In this attitude, elements characteristic of the non-recognition of a State are to be seen. From the legal standpoint the 'international existence' of the subject concerned is contested. From the political standpoint, hostility to that subject is expressed.

The political aspect of recognition or non-recognition was confirmed, if confirmation were needed, by subsequent changes of attitude, exchanging 'recognition' of the Communities against 'recognition' of the Council for Mutual Economic Assistance (Comecon) and a number of commercial advantages.

From 1977 to 1980, meetings took place in Brussels, Moscow and Geneva between an official EEC delegation (Commission) and an official Comecon delegation and its Member States. Nothing emerged from these meetings.

Subject to later comments on Romania, the position taken by the Soviet Union and the East European States is still based, therefore, on the original attitude of no *de jure* recognition.[2]

Against this, no State has as yet expressly recognized the Communities.[3]

There are grounds for thinking, however, that the establishment of diplomatic relations with the Communities, in the forms described in the following section, is equivalent to recognition, as in the case of a State.

There is no doubt that the sole fact of such establishment amounts to recognition of the Communities as a subject of international law. In our view, it also implies recognition

---

[1] Declaration at the International Wheat Conference, 18.1.1971.

[2] The *de facto,* and no longer the *de jure,* situation is different: 'The USSR is very well aware of the *de facto* situation which has arisen in Western Europe, including the existence of an economic association of capitalist countries in a common market' (speech by L. Brezhnev to the Trade Union Congress of the Soviet Union, 1972). On change in the Soviet attitude see, in particular, Ch. Zorgbibe, *L'Europe de l'Est face au Marché commun,* Colin, Paris, 1970; Ranson, *The European Community and Eastern Europe,* London, 1973; E. Wellenstein, '*The relations of the European Communities with Eastern Europe*', in: Essays in European Law and Integration, Kluwer, 1982, pp.197-208.

[3] In 1972, the People's Republic of China indicated that it was prepared 'to grant the EEC the degree of recognition it might wish to propose'. Nothing resulted from this proposal. In 1979, however, the People's Republic of China established a diplomatic mission to the Communities and this is equivalent to recognition.

of the international powers of the Communities as defined by the Treaties and resultant practice.[1]

In other words, any non-member country which has established diplomatic relations with the Communities should in good faith accept the consequences of its act and agree to deal only with the Communities in areas for which they have sole competence.[2]

It remains to be considered whether acts other than the establishment of diplomatic relations and in particular the conclusion of treaties can be equivalent to recognition.

At first sight they cannot. Under the general theory of recognition, the conclusion of an international agreement is not equivalent to recognition, even when the act is not qualified by any reservation on this point.

Indeed, some East European States have concluded limited agreements with the Communities without thereby changing their attitude in principle.[3]

However, the question takes on a special character in the case of Romania.

In 1980, that country did in fact conclude two agreements with the EEC, which were much wider in scope than those concluded with other East European States as they comprised a trade agreement and an agreement to set up a permanent body to maintain contacts between the EEC and Romania.[4]
Furthermore, the preamble to the second of these two agreements contains a paragraph worded as follows: 'Considering the powers vested in the EEC by the Treaty establishing it'.

Although Romania did not take the parallel further step of establishing a mission to the Communities in Brussels, it may be asked whether the conclusion of such agreements does not of necessity imply recognition of Community powers at least in the matter of external commercial relations.

---

[1] Such recognition should also normally apply to the geographical sphere of competence. Hence, the Communities do not accept the attitude of certain States which contest the application of Community competence to West Berlin. (On this question, see Part Three, pp.129-131.) As a result of this attitude, the Community has itself taken measures against such States when it has been able to do so, as it has against developing countries by making recognition of the Community with the geographical boundaries defined by the Rome Treaty a condition of Community aid. (At the end of 1982, Angola and Mozambique withdrew their reservation on Berlin in order to be able to benefit from the aid programme for non-associated developing countries and to take part in the negotiations for the renewal of the Lomé Convention.)

[2] Without prejudice to later discussion elsewhere in this study of the problems which arise when 'competence is shared' between the Community and its Member States or there are doubts as to where competence lies. In practice, any interest so far shown by non-member countries has mainly been directed to trade agreements. There can be no doubt that these come within the area of Community competence.

[3] See Part Two, pp. 62 and 63.

[4] Agreement of 28.7.1980 between the EEC and Romania on trade in industrial products (OJ L 352, 1980). Agreement of the same date on the establishment of a Joint Committee (same OJ).

B – Consequences of non-recognition of the Communities

Non-recognition can have awkward consequences as regards contractual relationships. It cannot have the same effect on the Communities' capacity to take 'autonomous' measures.

1. Non-recognition and contractual relationships

Practice in the matter of recognizing a State or government is extremely flexible.

It is an established fact that non-recognition never prevents the establishment of contacts or even the conclusion of international agreements.

In this respect, a sufficient example is provided by the extremely complex and detailed relations established between the German Democratic Republic and the Federal Republic of Germany when the latter completely denied the international existence of the former and even went as far as to break off diplomatic relations with States which recognized it ('Hallstein doctrine').

In the case of the Communities, the attitude of the Soviet Union did not prevent the eventual establishment of official contacts.

Nor did it prevent the conclusion of sectoral agreements with a number of East European States.[1]

Nevertheless, the attitude of the Soviet Union and the East European States has hitherto hampered the international activity of the Communities as regards both bilateral and multilateral relations.

The practical effect of non-recognition of the Communities is to deny the transfer of powers from the Member States to the Communities. It therefore puts the Member States in the difficult position of having, if they wish to adhere to their principles, to refuse to enter into contractual relationships with non-member countries in areas covered by transferred powers or to have recourse to *ad hoc* machinery which inevitably means departing from those principles. The question of trade relations with Eastern Europe clearly goes to the heart of its problems.

---

[1] See Part Two, pp. 64, 65, 70.

This has forced the Communities and the Member States to adopt solutions dictated largely by experience.[1]

In the case of multilateral relations, the effective consequences of the attitude of States which do not recognize the Communities have been more variable and have depended on the extent to which those States have been able to impose their view.

There can be no doubt, however, that most of the Communities' difficulty in gaining access to international conferences or to certain international legal instruments is due to the fact that, in this specific matter, the line taken by the East European States has stemmed logically from their attitude of principle to the Communities.

This further confirms, therefore, our finding relating to every subject of international law, which states that, while the theory of recognition may be extremely flexible, the fact that a subject of international law is not recognized by others always causes difficulties at some time or other.

2. Non-recognition and 'autonomous measures'

The non-recognition of a subject of law by others does not affect its 'objective' existence or its capacity to take measures within its powers.

Thus, assuming that a State is not recognized by any other (so far purely hypothetical), it is obvious that this clearly embarrassing situation does not prevent that State from exercising effective control over its territory and its citizens.

International organizations also have objective powers.

In the case of the Communities these powers are particularly wide.

In fact, because of the extent of their powers to make regulations and of the areas of competence transferred to them by the States, the Communities have powers of the same nature as those of States in respect of 'Community territory' and 'nationals of the Community'.

Inevitably, these powers affect third parties in one way or another, without their being able to challenge them. This is particularly true in the case of commercial relations.

---

[1] These solutions are not described in detail here. It is simply noted that, despite the expiry on 31.12.1969 of the 'transitional period' designated in the EEC Treaty, Member States were able, until the end of 1972, to sign trade agreements with the East European countries. As from 1.1.1975, when most of the trade agreements between Member States and those countries expired, the EEC and the ECSC introduced 'autonomous' arrangements for the import of products originating from those countries. In the case of 'EEC' products, the arrangement is at present governed by the regulations adopted by the Council of the Communities on 30.6.1982 (OJ L 195, 1982) and 14.11.1983 (OJ L 346, 1983). In addition, Member States are still authorized to sign 'cooperation agreements' with the East European countries, subject to monitoring by the Community (Council Decision of 22.7.1974, OJ L 208, 1974).

Thus, every product imported into the Community from West or East is subject to the rules (customs tariff, rules regarding origin, etc.) adopted by the Community organs.

These rules automatically apply unless the non-member State concerned has secured contractual exemption.

The specific consequences of the refusal by the East European States, on grounds of principle, to conclude such agreements with the Communities are that commercial relations with those States are basically subject to the autonomous measures adopted by the Communities.[1]

Clearly, the objective existence of the Communities and their capacity for independent action cannot be confined to the field of trade.

Thus, the competition rules laid down in the Treaty and implemented by regulation apply to all economic operators whose activites come within the competence of the Community in some way. The Court of Justice of the Communities has stated this principle very clearly with regard to non-European undertakings.[2]

Similarly, the maritime arrangements adopted by the Communities (exclusive economic zone), in the exercise of genuinely 'territorial' powers, are of universal application. In other words, a non-member State could not claim to be unaware of the existence of such zones on the grounds that it does not recognize the Communities.

Of course, when adopting such autonomous measures, the Communities, like a State, must observe the general principles of international law or the rules established by international conventions or treaties.

Non-member countries are moreover fully aware of this because they have already several times complained to GATT about autonomous EEC commercial measures.[3]

---

[1] Autonomous trade measures are not confined, however, to cases where they replace an agreement which could not be concluded.
The Communities began, for example, by introducing autonomous arrangements which were specially favourable to certain non-member countries. One of these is the generalized system of preferences (GSP). Another is the system of financial aid operated by the EEC since 1976 to assist developing countries in Asia and Latin America which are 'not associated' with the Community.
An autonomous measure can also be used to supplement an agreement or an arrangement similar to an agreement. This has been the case when the Community has entered into commitments and the method of implementation has been more or less left to its discretion. In this context, the purpose of an autonomous measure may be to grant the partner more favourable terms than those originally agreed. Another purpose may be to enable the Community to invoke safeguard clauses in the agreement.

[2] See ECR 14.2.1972, Joined Cases 48, 49, 51 and 57/69 *Dyestuffs* [1972] ECR 619; 21.2.1973, Case 6/72 *Continental Can* [1973] ECR 215.

[3] Quantitative restrictions or measures having an equivalent effect, the imposition of anti-dumping duties or the use of safeguard clauses provided for in agreements. In almost all cases, these disputes have been settled by negotiation.

Similarly, if any maritime measures adopted by the Communities ran completely counter to the generally accepted rules of international law, such action would be disciplined by the fact that the Communities could be held accountable, or even that non-member countries could this time legitimately claim that the regulations in question could not be argued against them in law. This demurrer would however be the simple consequence of an illegal act. It would have nothing to do with the recognition or non-recognition of the Communities.

Section 2: Recognition 'by' the European Communities

In the matter of recognition, international organizations play an indirect but important role.

Firstly, by acknowledging a new State or accepting the accreditation of a delegation to itself, an international organization implicity 'recognizes' the existence of the State concerned or the representative character of the organ and allows it to enter into what is today an important part of international relations.

Secondly, the attitude of certain organizations – at least of the largest of them, the United Nations – obviously has a major influence on its member States' decision to recognize or not recognize; to mention only two cases, China and Southern Rhodesia clearly illustrate this point.[1]

In this respect, the position of the Communities differs from that of the other organizations.

Firstly, whereas the UN, for example, implicitly recognizes a State by admitting it to membership, or a government does so by accepting its delegation,[2] the Communities behave like a State and establish diplomatic relations with such a non-member country by a procedure comparable to that used by States (see further on, Chapter II).[3]

Thus, the Community which originally approved the accreditation to it of a mission appointed by Taipeh but, in fact, established relations with the People's Republic of China, thereby implicity recognized the Beijing Government as entitled to represent the Chinese State.

---

[1] When the American hostages were held in Iran, the European Parliament adopted a resolution calling on the governments of Member States to consider breaking off diplomatic relations with Iran. This resolution had no practical results.

[2] The Community could be faced with this problem if several powers disputed the right to represent a Member State.

[3] Such relations established by agreement between the partners could be 'planned' by decision of either.

However, while practice for the establishment of 'diplomatic' relations shows marked similarities with the State procedure, the Communities have so far refrained from any *formal* decision to recognize a State or government. There is one exception, however.

The Community reacted simultaneously in two ways to the unilateral decision of the Turkish community in Cyprus to set up a 'Turkish Republic of North Cyprus'.

Firstly, the Ten issued the following statement on 16 November 1983 in the framework of political cooperation.

'The 10 Member States of the European Community are deeply concerned by the proclamation of an independent 'Turkish Republic of North Cyprus'. They reject this proclamation which is contrary to the successive resolutions of the United Nations. The Ten reaffirm their unconditional support for the independence, sovereignty, territorial integrity and unity of the Republic of Cyprus. They continue to regard the government of President Kyprianou as the sole legitimate government of the Republic of Cyprus. They call on all interested parties not to recognize this act, which creates a disturbing situation in the area.'

Secondly, the Commission issued the following statement the same day.

'The Commission greatly regrets and rejects the unilateral declaration of independence by the Turkish community in Cyprus. The government of the Republic of Cyprus is the sole lawful representative and the *sole representative recognized by the European Community.* The Commission, which is still anxious to implement the objectives of the association agreement between the Republic of Cyprus and the European Community, calls on the interested parties to reconsider the decisions just taken.'

The first statement represents a collective decision not to recognize, taken by the States themselves.

The second is a new departure since it represents the expression by the Community, as such, of powers to pronounce on the recognition or non-recognition of a State.

Unquestionably, however, this move forward by the Community is principally attributable to Cyprus's particulary close relations with the Community and to the special interest of one Member State in that country.

This precedent – which is of undoubted importance – should therefore be used with caution.

Chapter II – The international representation of the Communities

A prerequisite for the entry of a subject of law into international negotiations is the use of organs empowered to represent it and recognized as such by the other subjects.

The fundamental question is to know whether and to what extent the Communities can enjoy the rights and privileges which States have built up to their advantage on the basis of an age-old practice.

These rights and privileges are firstly those giving access to permanent organs located outside their territory and which confer a highly effective protective status; these are the legations (Section 1).

But present-day diplomacy increasingly involves contacts established directly between central governments or through delegations set up for specific negotiations; these are the *ad hoc* contacts (Section 2).[1]

Section 1: Permanent contacts: the problem of the Communities' 'right of legation'

The right of legation enables a subject of international law to be represented to other subjects by a permanent specialized organ having a protective status laid down by international law. As far as States are concerned, this is a time-honoured right, which is now well codified by the two Vienna Conventions on diplomatic (1961) and consular (1963) relations. The underlying principles are voluntarism (a State is not required to establish diplomatic relations with another) *de facto* reciprocity (in practically every case, the 'active' right of legation, i.e. of being represented, is matched by the 'passive' right of legation, i.e. representation of the other subject) and the extent of the protective status.

---

[1] See H.G. Schermers, '*The Community's relations under public international law*', in Thirty years of Community law, the 'European Perspectives' series, 1981, pp.219-233.

For international organizations, the situation is different. States soon realized the value of being represented at international organizations, and this led to an extension of the right of legation which is exercised not via embassies but via 'Permanent missions' for the member States and 'Permanent observer missions' for non-member States. This practice was codified by the Vienna Convention of 14 March 1975 on the representation of States in their relations with international organizations of a universal character.[1]

The States did not, however, accept that international organizations could exercise a similar right on a reciprocal basis. Admittedly, such organizations may, with the agreement of the State concerned, establish liaison and information offices, but these cannot be compared with embassies.

It was foreseeable that this one-sidedness would have an effect on the Communities and explains why the 'passive' right of legation (A) and the 'active' right of legation (B) must be dealt with separately.

A – Representation of States to the Communities: the 'passive' right of legation

This representation varies in both meaning and extent depending on whether Member States or non-member States are involved.

1. Representation of Member States

Each Member State has established a 'Permanent Representation' to the Communities.

In terms of both size and status, the representation is similar to an embassy, indeed a very high-ranking embassy in the State hierarchy. In practice, these missions are always headed by a very senior and experienced figure and maintain a large and well-qualified staff.

The appointment of the head and of the members of the mission is not subject to any accreditation or approval procedure on the part of the Communities.

At first sight, the function of the permanent representations is clearly defined if the provisions of Article 6 of the Vienna Convention of 14 March 1975 are applied. These state that:

---

[1] See Virally, Gerbet, Salmon, *Les missions permanentes auprès des organisations internationales,* 1971; J.J.A. Salmon, *Les représentations et missions auprès de la CEE et d'Euratom,* Brussels, 1971.

The functions of the permanent mission consist *inter alia* in:

(i) ensuring the representation of the sending State to the organization;
(ii) maintaining liaison between the sending State and the organization;
(iii) negotiating with and within the organization;
(iv) ascertaining activities in the organization and reporting thereon to the government of the sending State;
(v) ensuring the participation of the sending State in the activities of the organization;
(vi) protecting the interests of the sending State in relation to the organization;
(vii) promoting the realization of the purposes and principles of the organization by cooperating with and within the organization.

Each of the above provisions applies to the permanent missions of the Member States to the Communities.

However, the specific nature of the permanent missions of the Member States to the Communities is attributable to the part played by the permanent representatives (and the structure dependent on them) in the internal functioning of the Communities through the 'Permanent Representatives Committee' and its associated organs.

This role is subject to the internal institutional law of the Communities and is not within the province of external relations. Consequently, no further mention will be made of it here.

2. Representation of non-member States

The specific nature of the Communities compared with other organizations is clearly shown in both the function of the mission and its conditions of establishment.

(a) Functions of the mission

A non-member State is generally represented at an international organization by an observer mission.

The above-mentioned Vienna Convention defines the functions of the permanent observer mission as follows:

'Article 7: – ensuring the representation of the sending State and safeguarding its interests in relation to the organization and maintaining liaison with it;
– ascertaining activities in the organization and reporting thereon to the Government of the sending State;
– promoting cooperation with the organization and negotiating with it.'

In point of fact, the essential role of an observer mission to an organization is to inform the sending State about the activities of that organization and, where appropriate, to inform the organization of the problems which its activities may create for the sending State. Observer status generally allows members of the mission to attend meetings of the constituent organ of the organization and to speak, without of course being able to take part in the decision-making process.

Non-member States establish 'permanent missions' to the Communities (or 'delegations' in the case of ACP States).

The terms 'observers' and 'observation' have therefore been expunged from the Community vocabulary.

Whereas the missions of non-member States undeniably perform both an active and passive information role, they may not do so 'from the inside' by participating in the deliberations of the various organs.

Their activity is thus truly 'external' in relation to the organization, and this explains why they resemble more a traditional embassy than an observer mission.

Moreover, in view of the wide-ranging contractual powers conferred upon the Communities – generally exercised for and in place of those of their Member States – the main value of the mission for a non-member State is to maintain links with the Communities for the purposes of, or with a view to, negotiations with it (principally in the commercial field).

This is a further characteristic which, relatively speaking, brings relations with the Communities closer to relations with a State.

(b) Conditions for the establishment of a mission

A State has no right to establish an observer mission to an international organization. In practice, the prerequisite is that the State – or possibly a subject of a different kind – has been accepted as an observer to the organization which, in turn, is dependent on a decision by the competent organs of that organization.

Once this status has been acquired, however, the non-member State is not required to obtain the organization's consent for the actual formation of its mission or for the appointment of its head. It is merely required to notify this appointment to the Secretary-General (or the Director-General) of the organization. It is then incumbent on the head of the mission to submit his credentials to the Secretary-General or Director-General.[1]

This procedure has therefore very little in common with the procedure for accrediting a diplomatic mission to a State.

---

[1] Articles 9, 10 and 15 of the Vienna Convention of 14 March 1975. For further details about the absence of 'accreditation' to the United Nations, see Leo Gross, '*The UN and the role of law*', in International Organizations, 1961, and an opinion by the United Nations Legal Adviser in the United Nations Juridical Yearbook, 1964, p.234.

On the other hand, Community practice has been strongly influenced by national practice.

Generally speaking, the establishment of a mission to the Communities closely resembles the accreditation procedure used by States, in that non-member States must first obtain the agreement of the Community on the actual principle of establishing a mission.[1]

The next stage is that the State unofficially seeks the Communities' agreement on the person proposed to head the mission.

Once this agreement has been given, the prospective head has to submit his credentials.

Influenced by ECSC practice, under which the High Authority has sole responsibility for representation abroad,[2] and prompted by its desire to assert itself in this field, the Commission, with the Council's agreement,[3] originally played the dominant role concerning the passive right of legation. Until 1966, the credentials of heads of mission were presented solely to the President of the Commission in a State-type ceremonial.

Since then, however, there has been a new agreement between the two institutions,[4] under which credentials must be submitted simultaneously and separately to the President of the Commission and to the President-in-Office of the Council. With this new agreement, the ceremonial was simplified. This change, which was brought about entirely by internal factors, has in no way altered the procedure which is still that of accrediting a foreign mission.[5]

The missions of non-member States to the Communities enjoy diplomatic privileges and immunities by virtue of Article 17 of the Protocol on the Privileges and Immunities of the Communities. This article states that the Member States on whose territory the Communities have their seat shall grant the diplomatic privileges and immunities stemming from common law to the missions of non-member States accredited to the Communities. This is an actual provision for third parties of which the non-member States are, where appropriate, entitled to take advantage.

---

[1] However, for reasons not based on logic but on a desire to give express satisfaction to the States in question, it was agreed with respect to Greece when it had associate status and later with respect to Turkey and the AASM States (now the ACP States) that they did not have to obtain the prior agreement of the Communities on the principle of opening a 'delegation' or 'representation' or on the person who was to be its head.

[2] This practice still continues in that credentials concerning the ECSC are submitted to the President of the Commission only, cf. Commission reply published in the OJ of 9.9.1968, p.78 *et seq.*

[3] Exchange of letters of 25.7.1959 between the President of the Council and the President of the Commission supplemented by a formal regulation applicable at the opening and closure of a mission of a non-member State to the EEC.

[4] Commission/Council Agreement of November 1966 under the EEC and EAEC Treaties.

[5] The Commission publishes a yearbook of the 'Diplomatic Corps accredited to the European Communities'. Note that the missions of non-member States to the Communities are often composed of the same persons and especially the same head as the missions accredited to the Kingdom of Belgium.

B – *Representation of the Community to States: the 'active' right of legation*

1. Representation in Member States

There is no organ representing the Communities in their Member States.[1] The permanent representation – an organ of the State – acts as principal intermediary for the Community with the Member State.

This is not an exclusive role, however, as the Member States accept a whole series of direct relations between Community institutions (in particular, the Commission) and national authorities.[2]

2. Representation to non-member States

The ECSC exercised an active right of legation in the United Kingdom. Under the terms of an exchange of letters between the President of the High Authority and the United Kingdom representative to the ECSC, an ECSC delegation was established in London. The Head of the Delegation was accredited to the United Kingdom Government and not to the Court of St James. However, this difference does not appear to have resulted in his being given any special treatment. The Head of the ECSC Delegation was treated as an ambassador.

This practice gave rise to serious proposals at the end of the 1950s to establish similar delegations of the three Communities to a number of States, in particular the United Kingdom and the United States.

The Council, acting on proposals from the EEC and EAEC Commissions, took a decision in principle along these lines on 1 and 2 February 1960.

This initiative never materialized however, despite pressure from the European Parliament which took the view that the European Communities enjoyed both an active and passive right of legation by virtue of their international legal personality.[3]

---

[1] The Commission may, with the agreement of the Member States, establish Press and Information Offices in those States. The role of these offices is to inform public opinion in the Member States about the Communities' activities but they may not be treated as embassies from either the operational or statutory points of view.

[2] In order to inform the Member States about the initiatives taken by the Commission, paragraph 1 of the Resolution of 29.1.1966 adopted by the Extraordinary Council in Luxembourg (known as the 'Heptalogue' or seven-member Council) stipulated that: 'Before adopting a proposal of special importance, the Commission should make the appropriate contacts with the governments of the Member States through the intermediary of the permanent representatives without such procedure prejudicing the right of initiative which the Commission derives from the Treaty'. This resolution was never formally accepted by the Commission.

[3] EP Resolution of 17.11.1960: OJ, 16.12.1960, p.1496.

Since then, however, the Commission (with the implicit approval of the Council because the necessary budget funds were authorized) has established delegations in a number of States[1] which generally afford them the same treatment (see p.36) as the diplomatic missions of States.

From the standpoint of the active right of legation, there is a difference, since the diplomatic missions of States represent them in all aspects of their activity, whereas Commission delegations are naturally restricted to matters within Community competence.

The Member States, in turn, collectively entrust a number of diplomatic functions to the mission of whichever country is holding the presidency of the Council of the Communities at a given time. This is particularly true of questions concerning 'political cooperation'.

The ill-defined distribution of powers within the Community can lead to conflicts in the allocation of duties between the Commission delegate and the delegate of the State holding the presidency.

A Commission delegation to a non-member State is established once the State in question has given its agreement or at least registered no opposition after having been consulted.

The Head of Mission designate (after the Commission has unofficially sought the opinion of the government of the State concerned about the appointment) sends a letter of introduction to the Minister for Foreign Affairs. This letter is signed by the President of the Commission or the Member responsible for external relations.

The accreditation procedure is therefore less formal than the one used among the States themselves since the Heads of Mission generally submit their credentials to the Head of State.

The ACP States are a special case in that a provision of a protocol annexed to the Lomé Convention (Article 31 of Protocol No 2) provides for the establishment of Commission delegations.

Not only do these delegations play the usual role of liaison but they also help 'on the ground' with the implementation of Community policy towards these States. Their essential role in this respect is to oversee the proper execution of projects financed by the European Development Fund (EDF).

The Community delegations to non-member States enjoy privileges and immunities.

---

[1] At present the Commission has 13 delegations of this type (Algeria, Australia, Canada, Egypt, Israel, Japan, Jordan, Lebanon, Morocco, Syria, Tunisia, USA, Yugoslavia). It also has three regional delegations, Caracas for Latin America (with a branch office in Santiago), Bangkok for South-East Asia and New Delhi for South Asia (with a branch office in Dhaka).

In view of the continuing reluctance to accept that there is an unwritten rule obliging all States to grant privileges and immunities to missions and also that the privileges and immunities of the United Nations and its specialized agencies are based on multilateral conventions, bilateral agreements and unilateral acts of the States concerned, express provisions have ensured that these privileges and immunities have been granted to the Commission delegations. They are the result either of an agreement between the State concerned and the Community (e.g. Japan, Chile, ACP States) or of a unilateral act.[1]

In view of the diverse nature of these legal bases, there may be differences in the extent of the privileges and immunities granted.[2] Nevertheless, they are, on the whole, consistent with the common law on privileges and immunities which has gradually developed. They therefore apply both to the mission staff and to its premises, archives and communications.

It may be considered that, in establishing their 'delegations' the Communities are exercising, with the tacit agreement of the Member States and of the non-member host States, a right of legation which is not completely assimilable to States' right of legation. When the terms 'right of legation' or 'diplomatic representation' are used with reference to the Communities, the special circumstances in which they are exercised must be borne in mind.[3]

Section 2: 'Ad hoc' contacts

The advances made in means of communication have led to a situation today where one of the key components of diplomacy – apart from the straightforward telephone conversation – is the *meeting* at which one or more questions may be discussed.

Such meetings take place continually at various levels, i.e. senior officials often from the 'specialized' ministries and not from the Foreign Ministries, ministers and finally Heads of State or Government.

In the case of the specialized meetings, the public is not generally informed but if the meeting is at ministerial level – and *a fortiori* at summit level – it usually ends with the publication of a text variously referred to as: communiqué, declaration, proceedings, etc.

---

[1] e.g.: United States, Executive Order of 5.12.1972; Canada, Order of 2.10.1975.

[2] One author has pointed out that with the ACP States, the privileges and immunities were more limited than the usual diplomatic privileges and immunities since they were granted 'solely in the interests of official duties'. This would suggest that no protection is given to diplomats in their private lives but, in practice, this provision is not enforced to the letter (E. Sauvignon, '*Les Communautés européennes et le droit de légation actif*', Revue du Marché commun, 1978, p.176).

[3] For example, P. Pescatore writes that 'The characteristic of the diplomatic mission is thus at the same time of such a general and essentially political nature that it has been described by the Latin expression *jus repraesentationis omnimodo*' ('*Les relations extérieures des Communautés*', Recueil des cours de l'*Académie de droit international,* RCADI, Vol. 103, p.191).

A meeting may involve two partners, in which case it would be referred to as 'bilateral' diplomacy, still the most common form of contact. But it may also involve several partners, in which case it will be referred to as 'plurilateral' diplomacy although this is not fundamentally different from the bilateral type.

A meeting may, however, be open to a larger number of partners and in this case 'multilateral' diplomacy is involved either at international conferences specially convened to discuss a particular topic (recent examples being the Paris Conference of 1975-77 on International Economic Cooperation, the Helsinki and Geneva Conferences of 1973 and 1975 on Security and Cooperation in Europe), or in permanent international organizations.

Such bodies provide both the 'stage' and the 'actors'[1] for *ad hoc* diplomacy. The higher the political profile of these bodies, the more their actions will register with public opinion, especially when carried out at the highest level.

To take one of the best-known examples, no one is today surprised at the diplomatic activity of the Secretary-General of the United Nations. On the contrary, it seems quite normal that the Secretary-General should act in a personal capacity, particularly at meetings with Heads of State or Government, in pursuit of the organization's mission concerning the peaceful settlement of disputes.

Similarly, the role of the European Communities as an 'actor' in *ad hoc* diplomacy is also fully recognized.

At its most discreet, this activity involves the participation of Community officials and experts in myriad meetings of either a bilateral, plurilateral or multilateral nature with their counterparts in non-member countries.

The international activity of the Communities takes on particular importance when their most senior representatives meet ministers, Heads of State or Government of non-member countries.

The question of the Communities' international representation arises in all these manifestations of *ad hoc* diplomacy. Quite clearly, this question is the sole responsibility of the Communities, and the solutions are linked to the nature of the powers involved.

When discussions or negotiations with non-member countries are concerned solely with problems falling *stricto sensu* within the purview of a particular Community, it is normally represented by the Commission. In 1978, for example, the Commission President, Mr Roy Jenkins, paid an official visit to Japan (where he was received by the Emperor), the purpose of the visit being to discuss commercial relations between Japan and the EEC. Similarly, it is the members or senior officials of the Commission who repre-

---

[1] These expressions are taken from J.L. Dewost and D. Vignes, writing in *Organisations européennes et vie internationale,* (European organizations and international life), proceedings of the Nancy colloquium (1981) of the French International Law Society, Pedone 1982, p. 219 *et seq.*

sent the EEC on the management bodies responsible for the bilateral trade agreements between the Community and various non-member countries[1] and in the less formal structures set up to provide a dialogue with other countries, also to discuss commercial and economic questions.[2]

When the discussions or negotiations with non-member countries deal with foreign policy questions coming under the 'political cooperation' arrangements between the Member States of the Communities but are outside the Community framework, the international representation of the group comprising these States is the responsibility of whichever State holds the presidency of the Council of the European Communities and, depending on the circumstances is the responsibility of this country's Head of State or Government, its ministers or less senior officials.[3]

It frequently happens at international meetings of a bilateral, plurilateral or multilateral nature that international-level representation of a particular European Community and national-level representation of one of its constituent Member States have to be provided simultaneously.

This is especially true when the meeting has to deal both with questions for which the Community is competent and questions relating to 'political cooperation'. The best-known example is that of the periodic Western 'summits' (Rambouillet (1975), Versailles (1982), Williamsburg (1983), London (1984)) of the Heads of State or Government of the main industrialized countries (i.e. the United States, Canada, Japan, the Federal Republic of Germany, France, Italy, the United Kingdom). Since 1978, both the President of the Commission and the President-in-Office of the Council of the European Communities have attended these summits. For the same reasons, there is dual representation of the EEC (by the Commission) and of its Member States at the periodic meetings with the member countries of Asean (Indonesia, Malaysia, Philippines, Singapore, Thailand), which deal not only with the implementation of the 1980 commercial cooperation agreement between these countries and the EEC, but also with international policy issues of mutual concern.

The practice adopted for meetings within the framework of the Euro-Arab Dialogue[4] has also been used for the periodic meetings with Latin American countries.

The Communities' international activities, even when limited to economic questions, often involve both the powers of the Communities (especially the EEC) and those re-

---

[1] In particular, the 'Joint Committees' set up under the trade agreements concluded by the EEC in 1972-73 with all the members of the European Free Trade Association, see Part Two, p. 64.

[2] The reference here is to the high level bilateral meetings every six months or each year which have brought together members or senior officials of the Commission and members or representatives of the governments of the United States, Japan, Canada, Australia, South Korea and the People's Republic of China.

[3] For example, during the summer of 1980 following the European Council in Venice, the President-in-Office of the Council went on a fact-finding mission to the Middle East to brief the Nine (Greece was not yet a member of the Communities) on what form an initiative by them could take.

[4] W. Hantke, 'The specialized group of general contract conditions within the Euro-Arab dialogues', Common Market Law Review, 1981, pp.197-203.

tained by the Member States although, for either legal or political reasons which we will return to later,[1] it is impossible to distinguish any dividing line.

This situation explains why many bilateral or multilateral international agreements have been concluded with non-member countries not solely by the Community ('Community agreements'),[2] but simultaneously by the Community and its Member States under the 'mixed agreement' procedure[3] and that, consequently, the delegation representing the European component in the bodies administering these agreements (e.g. the EEC-Turkey Association Council, the Cooperation Councils set up by the agreements between the EEC and the Maghreb States, the ACP-EEC Council of Ministers and the ACP-EEC Committee of Ambassadors established by the Lomé Conventions) is made up of both EEC representatives (Commission) and of representatives of each of the Member States.

The same situation accounts for the dual representation of the Community and its Member States in the deliberative organs of international organizations and conferences, in respect of which the Community – under complex conditions which will be described in Part One Chapter III of this study[4] – has a right of access and participation. No less complex are the arrangements which the Community and its Member States have made to provide this dual representation, since they are entirely independent of any action which may be taken by third country members of the organizations or conferences in question although as Chapter III points out, the 'recognition' of the Community's right of access and participation is dependent on the goodwill of these third countries.

To date, basically four types of arrangement have been used.[5]

The first involves the establishment of a Community delegation composed solely of Commission representatives and Council officials, each Member State having its own delegation.[6]

The second also involves a Community delegation, which is separate from the individual Member States' delegations, but comprises not only Commission representatives and Council officials, but also one or more representatives of the State holding the Council presidency.[7]

---

[1] See Part Two, p. 59.

[2] In particular, the trade agreements concluded by the EEC with the member countries of the European Free Trade Association (EFTA). A list of the main 'Community' agreements is given in Part Two, pp. 61-64.

[3] A list of the main 'mixed' agreements is given in Part Two, pp.62-65. Part Two also contains further details about the basis and extent of the distinction between 'Community' and 'mixed' agreements.

[4] See p.41.

[5] See J. Groux, 'Mixed Negotiations' in Mixed Agreements (collected texts edited by D. O'Keefe and H.G. Schermers, Kluwer, 1983, pp.87-96).

[6] It was this arrangement which was used in the negotiations at the Third United Nations Conference on the Law of the Sea (1973-82).

[7] This second arrangement is used to provide EEC representation to the United Nations General Assembly. It was also used in the negotiation of the Tin and Coffee Agreements, see Part Two p. 62.

The third arrangement differs from the previous one in that the Community delegation, again separate from the Member States' delegations, includes not only Commission representatives, Council officials, representatives of the Member State holding the presidency of the Council, but also representatives of each of the other Member States.[1]

The fourth arrangement differs from all the others, in that it involves the setting up of a single delegation for both the Community and its Member States, under which the latter no longer have any individual delegations, but their representatives are included in the single delegation alongside the Commission representatives and the Council officials.[2]

The single delegation arrangement is undoubtedly the one which can ensure the best cohesion of the Community and its Member States.

---

[1] This third arrangement was used in the negotiation of the Cocoa and Natural Rubber Agreements, see Part Two p. 62.

[2] Known as the 'Rome' formula, this arrangement was used for the 1967 cereals negotiations which took place in Rome following the multilateral trade negotiations of the Kennedy Round. It was again used at the Paris Conference on International Economic Cooperation (1975-77). Under the terms of a decision of the Council of the European Communities of 30.3.1981 (known as the 'PROBA 20' Decision), it must be used for the negotiations and preparatory work concerning the formulation, renewal and management of all the agreements on those commodities coming under the Unctad Integrated Programme of 1976 (excluding those agricultural products sold in the EEC under the common market organization).

Chapter III – The European Communities' access to, and participation in, the work of international organizations and conferences

Depending on the circumstances and the questions to be discussed, the United Nations Organization and its various institutions and specialized agencies, and many other international organizations or bodies of universal or regional character, whether permanent or temporary, cater in varying degree for the needs of multilateral cooperation.

The European Communities are themselves a focus of such cooperation, but many of their activities transcend the boundaries of their Member States.

To begin with, the European Communities have powers in a variety of fields (for example trade, development aid, environmental protection, transport, nuclear energy, etc.) in which their initiatives – like those of other countries or groups – cannot lead to any concrete achievements without the agreement and participation of varying numbers of external partners. Frequently, one or other of the existing international organizations is the appropriate framework for negotiations with these countries.

Secondly, some of the measures which the Communities may find it necessary to take may affect the interests of non-member countries and, failing a negotiated settlement, may lead to disputes which have to be settled by international organizations. The well-known example of GATT springs to mind, in the context of which the EEC has frequently been called upon to defend certain of its policies, particularly its agricultural policy, and also to protest against detrimental decisions taken by other parties.

These circumstances have led the European Communities not only to establish regular working contacts with the majority of permanent international organizations, but also and above all to claim a specific right of access to, and participation in, the work of the deliberative organs of these organizations and of certain *ad hoc* international conferences.

The Commission of the European Communities has, pursuant to the powers conferred upon it by Article 229 of the EEC Treaty,[1] concluded 'liaison agreements' with the executive organs of virtually all the existing world and regional organizations.[2]

These agreements are fairly homogeneous in content although different in formulation, and generally contain measures designed to promote contacts and exchanges of experience between the departments and staff of the signatory organizations, and to promote a two-way flow of information on their respective activities.[3]

The cooperation initiated by these liaison agreements has been strengthened by the setting up of permanent delegations of the Commission of the European Communities to those international organizations over whose work the Community has special reasons for exercising extremely close supervision. Such delegations have been established at the OECD in Paris, and at organizations with headquarters in New York (United Nations), Geneva (GATT; United Nations) and Vienna (OPEC; United Nations: Unido, IAEA).[4]

Generally speaking, the establishment of regular working relations between the Communities and other international organizations has not given rise to any particular problems.[5]

On the other hand, several problems have occurred over the assignment to the European Communities of a specific right of access to, and participation in, the work of international organizations and conferences.

---

[1] Article 229 states that it shall be for the Commission to 'ensure the maintenance of all appropriate relations with the organs of the United Nations, of its specialized agencies and of the General Agreement on Tariffs and Trade (GATT)' and shall also maintain 'such relations as are appropriate with all international organizations'. Similar provisions are contained in Article 93 of the ECSC Treaty and in Article 199 of the EAEC Treaty.

[2] A list of the organizations with which the Commission of the European Communities has concluded 'liaison agreements', together with the full texts of these agreements, are given in: *The European Community, international organizations and multilateral agreements,* second edition (1980), Office for Official Publications of the European Communities, Luxembourg. Additional references are: Agreement with the Council of Arab Economic Unity (OJ L 300, 1982); exchange of letters with the World Health Organization (OJ L 300, 1982); United Nations Programme for the Environment (OJ C 248, 1983); the International Commission on Civil Status (OJ L 260, 1983); International Centre for Advanced Mediterranean Agronomic Studies (OJ C 45, 1984).

[3] This information is especially useful to the European Commission in that it enables it to identify those questions likely to be of particular interest for the Community from among all the questions which the organizations with which the Commission has signed agreements are called upon to discuss. The Commission can thus draw on key information when advocating to the Council of the European Communities the positions which the Community might have to adopt during any discussions planned by the organization in question.

[4] One international organization – the Council of Europe – has, in turn, established a branch office to provide representation to the European Communities. Since 1975, it has had a permanent liaison office at the Council and the Commission of the European Communities.

[5] It should be remembered, however, that the negotiations conducted between 1975 and 1980 between the Communities and the Council for Mutual Economic Assistance (Comecon) produced neither a normalization of relations between the two organizations nor the establishment of basic working contacts.

The question now scarcely raises any difficulties concerning principles (Section 1). The manner in which the Communities can exercise their right of participation has also been very largely settled, even if they may still give rise to some controversy (Section 2) and do not entirely meet the requirements of the Communities' 'constitution' (Section 3).

Section 1: The question of principle

Is there a real need to confer upon the European Communities a separate right of access to, and participation in, the work of the deliberative organs of international organizations and conferences?

The fact that, in most cases, all the Community Member States are also members of the organization or conference and actively take part in their work might, at first sight, cast doubt on this need. Would it not be sufficient for these States to agree on the positions to be adopted, on behalf of the Community, within the organization or at the conference concerned and to agree among themselves how one or more of their number will state their case?

For both political and legal reasons, the European Communities believed that it would not be sufficient.

Under the rules and practices of international organizations and conferences, the admittance of any member (or other type of participant) is a discretionary and therefore political matter. Accordingly, the attribution to the European Communities of a separate status within the deliberative organ of international organizations and conferences necessarily involves the 'recognition' of their international existence and personality, a fact to which the European Communities quite naturally attach great importance.

No one has ever been in any doubt about this. In practice, the decision to allow any of the European Communities to have a seat at international organizations or at international conferences and to be given the right to exercise certain prerogatives there has often led to a political 'battle' between its supporters and opponents.

As far as the principles are concerned, this battle may now be considered as almost over since the great majority of permanent international organizations have officially allowed the Communities, and in particular the EEC, to take part in their proceedings. It is worth pointing out, however, that, in the case of the United Nations General Assembly, this right was not granted to the EEC until 1974 and then only after the same right had been granted simultaneously to the CMEA (Comecon).

The problem of conferring official status on the European Communities also arises whenever a temporary diplomatic conference is convened for specific negotiations, whether or not under the aegis of a permanent international organization.

On each occasion, the Communities must ensure that the decision convening the conference and the rules of procedure actually allow their representatives to take part.

As a general rule, they get satisfaction.

In this way, the EEC was granted the right to participate in the work of the Paris Conference on International Economic Cooperation (1975-77) and the Third United Nations Conference on the Law of the Sea (1973-82). On the other hand, it was not given the right to accredit representatives to the Conference on Security and Cooperation in Europe (Helsinki) and the ensuing conferences (Belgrade, Madrid). The only course open to its delegates was to attend, without separate identification, among the delegation of the State holding the presidency of the Council of the European Communities.[1]

The fact that the Communities do attach importance to being officially represented in the deliberations of international organizations and conferences is not only out of a desire for 'political' recognition, but is also and above all attributable to a legal necessity arising from the Treaties establishing them.

Only a few points need be noted concerning internal Community law:

1. The Court of Justice of the European Communities has clearly ruled that, when a commitment which is binding in international law is being entered into, in any form, in an international organization or conference and where that commitment will relate, wholly or in part, to matters concerning the powers transferred to the EEC, the latter is solely competent, to the exclusion of its Member States, to negotiate the commitment in question, in relation to these matters.[2]

2. The Treaty establishing the European Economic Community entrusted the Commission with the task of negotiating on its behalf all agreements and other binding commitments under international law.
Clearly, the Commission of the European Communities cannot carry out the task thus entrusted to it unless its representatives have official access to the negotiating bodies.

3. Article 116 of the EEC Treaty states: 'From the end of the transitional period onwards, Member States shall, in respect of all matters of particular interest to the common market, proceed within the framework of international organizations of an economic character only by common action. To this end, the Commission shall submit to the Council, which shall act by a qualified majority, proposals concerning the scope and implementation of such common action.'

This is not the place to comment upon provisions which still give rise to different interpretations, especially as regards the subject matter and types of international negotiations to which they might apply.

---

[1] Decision taken on 11.9.1973 in Copenhagen by the Foreign Ministers of the Nine, followed by an identical decision taken on 20.9.1973 by the Council of the European Communities.
[2] Opinion 1/78 of 4.10.1979, [1979] ECR 2871.

It need merely be pointed out that whereas implementation of the common action provided for by Article 116 is the responsibility of the Member States of the EEC as a whole and not of its institutions, it is the institutions which are responsible for formulating the content of such action.

It is difficult to see how the representatives of these institutions, in particular the Commission, could effectively take on this responsibility if they were excluded from the negotiating chamber and were unable to follow the discussions which could at any moment call for changes in the common position initially agreed.

Section 2: Ways and means for the participation of the Communities in the work of the deliberative organs of international organizations and conferences

In none of the international organizations which existed prior to the establishment of the Communities nor in any of the *ad hoc* conferences convened under the auspices of those organizations have the European Communities been recognized as a member on an equal footing with individual States. The reasons for this will be discussed and a description given of 'observer' status, which is the most the Communities have so far been able to achieve.

A – Non-recognition of the status of full member

The powers held by the Communities were vested in them by the transfer of powers from their Member States. They are therefore of the same nature as those of the Member States. Consequently, it could have been argued that these powers could be exercised within international organizations and conferences only if the Communities enjoyed the same prerogatives as the States, i.e., membership.

The Communities' claim for such status would undoubtedly have met with major obstacles.

In practice, the instruments establishing most, if not all, of the existing international organizations expressly confer the status of member on States. The same applies to the rules of procedure of *ad hoc* conferences convened under the auspices of these organizations, in particular the United Nations and its specialized agencies.

Extending the status of member to the Communities would therefore have meant a revision of these instruments or rules.

The chances of such an operation succeeding would doubtless have been fairly slim in view of the hostility of East European States to the Communities and the likely indifference of many other States towards a measure which would have meant infringing one of the basic 'constitutional' rules of such organizations or conferences.

Accordingly, the European Communities have so far generally refrained from seeking membership of existing international organizations or conferences convened under their auspices.

The Communities' attitude is less reserved towards international bodies recently established by either the transformation or remodelling of pre-existing bodies.

Application for membership by one of the European Communities to a newly-created body whose institutional rules are still to be defined may in practice encounter fewer problems than in the case of an existing body subject to fairly fixed statutory rules. Furthermore, the admittance of the Community as a member of a new body may be facilitated by the fact that the establishment of such an organization involved decisions on a whole range of problems among which this particular question may not be the most difficult. Finally, the fear of setting a precedent may not be as great in a new type of body as it is with an organization which already belongs to a family of institutions all governed by similar rules.

In point of fact, the EEC has in recent years been offered full member status with newly-created international bodies[1] dealing with questions in respect of which the EEC can claim special competence.

B – Observer status

Turning now to the many, important international institutions where the European Communities have only observer status, the circumstances in which this status was granted will be discussed; this will be followed by a description of the arrangements whereby this status enables them to participate in the work of the deliberative organs of the institutions concerned.

Granting of observer status

International organizations and conferences of a world-wide or regional character generally allow other intergovernmental organizations and other entities of a different character (non-independent territories, freedom movements, non-governmental organ-

---

[1] Examples: the International Energy Agency set up in 1975 under the auspices of the OECD; the North Atlantic Fisheries Organization (NAFO) which in 1978 replaced the International Commission for the Northeast Atlantic Fisheries (ICNAF), of which the EEC was not a member; the deliberative organs set up by the world commodity agreements to which the EEC became party (coffee, cocoa, tin, olive oil, natural rubber, etc.). Part Two of this study (p. 84 *et seq.*) will consider the specific problems which have arisen as a result of the EEC being given the right to participate as a member in the proceedings and sessions of these institutions.

izations) to participate as an observer in the work of their various institutions, when questions of special interest to these organizations and entities are discussed.[1]

The fact that this is possible is often not enough to ensure that a particular organization or entity actually participates.

The decision to invite an organization or entity to participate in the work of the international organization concerned is generally one which is beyond the competence of the latter's executive organs or secretariat,[2] especially when a standing invitation is involved. The decision therefore has to be taken by the deliberative assembly of the organization.

In view of the political nature of the criteria governing the granting of such rights, the right of participation by intergovernmental organizations and other entities may vary from one organization to another and, for many years, the Communities had very different oportunities for access to the various organizations whose work was of particular interest to them.

It was only gradually and after overcoming a number of hurdles, the details of which are not essential to this study,[3] that the Communities firmly established a specific right of participation in the work of most of these organizations.

It should be remembered that the Communities' status is nearly always that of observer with a right to take part in the meetings of the deliberative organs of the organization, but without the right to vote.

In some cases, the actual statutes of the organization (OECD) have made provision for the granting of this status. More frequently, however, it has resulted from an individual decision taken by the deliberative assembly of the organization concerned.[4]

---

[1] See for example: Article 75 of the Rules of Procedure of the United Nations Economic and Social Council; Article 12 of the 'Mandate' of the United Nations Economic Commission for Europe (ECE); Resolution 1995 (XIX) of 30.12.1964 concerning Unctad, etc. All these texts are contained in the work previously quoted: *The European Community, international organizations and multilateral agreements.*

[2] Note in particular that the 'liaison agreements' concluded by the Commission of the European Communities with the executive organs or secretariats of other international organizations make no reference to the Communities' participation in the sessions and work of the deliberative organs of these organizations. Historically, however, the signing of such agreements has nearly always been followed by the granting of an official right to the Communities to take part in the sessions and proceedings. On at least one occasion the secretariat of an international organization (WIPO in 1977) considered the signing of a liaison agreement as the prerequisite for the granting of this right to the EEC.

[3] On this and on other topics dealt with in this chapter, see in particular: G. Le Tallec, 'Quelques aspects des rapports entre la CEE et les organisations internationales', *Revue du Marché commun*, 1973, p. 636 *et seq;* J.P. Jacqué, *'La participation de la CEE aux organisations internationales universelles',* Annuaire français de droit international, 1975, p. 924 *et seq.*

[4] Examples are: Resolution 1267 (XLIII) of 3.8.1967 and the Decision of 20.5.1971 of the United Nations Economic and Social Council; Resolution 3208 (XXXIX) of 11.10.1974 of the United Nations General Assembly 'calling on the Secretary-General to invite the European Economic Community to participate as an observer in the sessions and work of the General Assembly'; Resolution of 15.4.1975 of the United Nations Economic Commission for Europe, etc.

All these texts are to be found in the work previously mentioned, i.e.: *The European Community, international organizations and multilateral agreements.*

The individual decisions taken with respect to the Communities confer upon them the separate right to participate – via a delegation of their choice accredited to the organization – in the sessions and work of the organization concerned.

The Communities do not enjoy permanent observer status with international organizations whose deliberative organs have not been called upon to rule on the case of the Communities. Their participation in the work of the organization still depends on invitations regularly sent to the Commission by the organization's secretariat with the express or tacit approval of that organization's deliberative body. This arrangement operates with the FAO, WHO and IMO (formerly IMCO).

Apart from this formal difference, the Communities' representatives enjoy virtually the same rights with the various international organizations.

At the present time, the EEC alone participates as a permanent observer – on either a *de jure* or *de facto* basis – in the proceedings and work of:

(i)   virtually all the institutions in the United Nations group: principal organs (General Assembly, Economic and Social Council), subsidiary organs (Unctad, regional commisions, in particular the Economic Commission for Europe), specialized agencies (ILO, FAO, Unesco, WHO, IMO, WIPO, IMF, Unido), International Atomic Energy Agency;

(ii) many other organizations of a universal character (Customs Cooperative Council) or regional character (OECD, Council of Europe, European Conference of Ministers of Transport, Central Commission for the Navigation on the Rhine, etc.).

Aspects of observer status

The main questions raised by the European Communities' enjoyment of observer status with the deliberative bodies of international organizations and conferences have in practice been as follows: establishment and prerogatives of Community delegations, right of Community representatives to attend and speak, right to table proposals and amendments, right to vote.

Community delegation

The European Communities' representatives at sessions of the deliberative bodies of international organizations and conferences form a delegation, the list of whose members is in each case communicated to the secretariat of the organization or conference. They are entered on the official list of delegations under the heading generally devoted to intergovernmental organizations.[1]

---

[1]   Obviously, the composition of the Community delegation is a matter for the Community alone. As described earlier (p. 39), the practice adopted by the Community has involved various 'formulae'.

The Community delegation normally has its own seat and name-plate.

The usual practice in almost all international organizations and conferences is that the national delegates sit at the alphabetically-arranged places assigned to their States, whereas the delegates from observer organizations (which include the Communities) sit in a part of the room separate from that set aside for national representatives. Notwithstanding this rule, the Community's efforts – particularly at Unctad[1] – to have its own delegates grouped in the same part of the conference room as its Member States' delegates have met with objections – especially from some Eastern European countries – which have still not been entirely removed.

Right of Community representatives to attend and speak

The right of Community representatives to attend meetings of the main and subsidiary deliberative bodies of international organizations and conferences is no longer a source of any major problem. When, however, the discussions take place during unofficial meetings or in working or contact groups, access to which – for reasons of effectiveness – is restricted to a few delegations, the Commission representatives are not always able to participate.

The right to speak is generally granted to observers without restriction, especially to the Community representatives. But some restrictive practices do also operate.

Thus, the EEC representatives may speak at meetings of commissions of the United Nations General Assembly but not in the Plenary Assembly itself.

In other organizations, observers have to be specially authorized to speak by the chairman of the meeting. Cases have occurred where pressure from some delegations has led to this authorization being refused to the Commission representatives or to its being granted only on a very limited basis. Such cases are now fairly rare.

Right to table proposals and amendments

The right of Community negotiators to table proposals or amendments on the Community's behalf to the texts under discussion continues to cause problems, especially in organizations where the Eastern European delegations carry particular weight such as in the United Nations Economic Commission for Europe.

The rules of procedure of international organizations and conferences are often silent or unclear about the rights of observers to table proposals or amendments; consequently, they can give rise to controversy.

---

[1] Pursuant to the 'PROBA 20' Decision of the Council of the European Communities of 30.3.1981 providing for the establishment of a single delegation of the EEC and its Member States for the negotiations and preparatory work regarding the drafting, renewal and administration of the agreements on commodities affected by the Unctad Integrated Programme of 1976 (see above, p. 39).

The United Nations Legal Service,[1] which has frequently been consulted on this question, has recognized that the EEC is an entity having its own personality and powers to negotiate distinct from those of its Member States and has concluded that it should be accorded a status appropriate to this situation within international organizations and conferences.

But it has yet to accept, however, that the Community may, in its own right, table proposals or amendments. The most that it has conceded is that EEC representatives should be authorized to table proposals or amendments on behalf of the Member States collectively.[2]

The Community's right to table proposals and amendments in its own right has not therefore been properly recognized so far.

The importance of this question should not be overestimated, however.

To begin with, part of the discussion which takes place at international organizations and conferences is no more than an exchange of views and does not relate to specific texts.

Secondly, when the discussion does deal with specific texts, the subjects dealt with seldom come within the sole competence *stricto sensu* of a particular European Community. All that is required in some cases is 'common action' by the Member States within the meaning of Article 116 of the EEC Treaty. In such cases, it is the collective responsibility of the Member States and not of the EEC to table proposals and amendments, so that the right of these institutions' representatives to table proposals or amendments cannot be questioned.

That being so, it is often very difficult to distinguish between subjects which require specifically Community action and those which require common action by the Member States. There are differences of view on this point between the Commission of the European Communities and the Member States and between the Member States themselves.

Moreover, it would certainly be undesirable if the European Communities and their Member States were constantly having to change spokesmen whenever the discussion switched from a subject requiring specifically Community action to a subject requiring common action by the Member States or vice versa.

---

[1] See Opinion of 15.11.1971, *United Nations Juridical Yearbook*, 1971, p. 206.

[2] The International Labour Office found it necessary to adopt a similar position in a document concerning the 'Relationship between the rights and obligations arising from the ILO Constitution and the rights and obligations arising from Treaties establishing Regional Groups (ILO Document GB. 215/SC/4/1/, February-March 1981). This document states, in particular, that 'there is nothing in the (ILO) rules to prevent a group of government delegates from authorizing the representative of a body to table amendments on their collective behalf; these amendments shall be treated as if they had been tabled by the government delegates concerned'.

50

The Communities and their Member States must of course respect the rules laid down by the Treaties establishing the Communities, but they must also adopt reasonable and practicable attitudes when putting forward their arguments.

Consequently, the Commission representative often intervenes in a discussion on topics in respect of which the Member States alone would normally be entitled to submit proposals or amendments, or the representative of the Member State holding the presidency of the Council of the European Communities speaks on subjects on which normally only the Commission representative is entitled to express an opinion. Use of the latter procedure is clearly unorthodox under Community law; on the other hand, it has the advantage of silencing delegations who consider that an organization or entity with mere observer status cannot table proposals or amendments to texts under discussion.

Thirdly, the crucial stages of negotiations taking place in international organizations and conferences usually occur during unofficial and informal meetings. These discussions are often based either on proposals which do not commit delegations officially or on compromise solutions worked out by the chairman or leader of the negotiating group after private consultations with particular delegations.

Formal rules of procedure are scarcely appropriate in such unofficial exchanges of view and, provided the Community representatives have something to say with which all the Member States agree, they are rarely prevented from submitting drafting proposals themselves, nor are they pressed to specify whether these proposals reflect the Community's position or that of the Member States collectively.

The right of Community representatives to table proposals or amendments on behalf of the Community is therefore only really questioned on relatively few occasions.

The question of the right to vote

As a general rule, organizations and entities with observer status to international organizations and conferences do not have the right to vote.[1]

There is no exemption from this rule for the European Communities, which means that even where questions within their competence are concerned, only the Member States are entitled, if appropriate, to cast a vote.

---

[1] See for example Article 79, already quoted, of the Ecosoc Rules of Procedure which state that: 'The representatives of intergovernmental organizations ... may participate, without the right to vote, in those proceedings of the Council which relate to the field of activity of these organizations'. Resolution 1995 (XIX), already quoted, states in connection with Unctad that: 'The Trade and Development Board may make provision for the representatives of intergovernmental bodies ... to participate, without the right to vote, in its proceedings and in those of any subsidiary bodies and working groups it may have established ...'.

Special cases

The aspects of observer status described in the preceding paragraphs could be said to reflect the 'average' position of the European Communities with respect to international organizations and conferences.

The EEC position is better than this average in the following three organizations: OECD, GATT and (incidentally) the World Food Council.

OECD

The OECD, it will be remembered, succeeded the OEEC, which was set up in 1948. Additional Protocol No 1 to the Convention establishing the OECD entitles the Commission of the European Communities to participate in the work of the organization.[1] It further provides that representation to the organization of the European Communities established by the Paris and Rome Treaties shall be ensured 'in accordance with the institutional provisions of these Treaties'.

Protocol No 1 is certainly not intended to confer upon the Communities the status of OECD member nor to give them the right to vote at its meetings, but it does ensure, in particular,[1] that they have every opportunity they require to submit proposals and amendments.

GATT

The European Communities' position within GATT is also highly favourable.[2] Although the EEC has, by virtue of Article 113 of its Treaty, assumed most of the functions relating to matters within the province of GATT (international trade regulations), it has not formally replaced its Member States as 'contracting parties' to GATT. These States remain bound by the General Agreement; they are required to approve any modifications which may, from time to time, be made to this Agreement and they participate individually in the financing of the organization's expenditure. They still sit in the deliberative organs of GATT and have their own name-plates but merely 'surround' the EEC delegation, whose right to speak and to table proposals and amendments in its own name is now fully recognized.

---

[1] '1. Representation to the OECD of the European Communities established by the Paris and Rome Treaties of 18.4.1951 and 25.3.1957 respectively, shall be regulated in accordance with the institutional provisions of these Treaties.
2. The EEC and EAEC Commissions and the High Authority of the ECSC shall participate in the work of this organization'.

[2] See J.H.J. Bourgeois, *'Le GATT et le traité CEE'*, Social Economische Wetgeving, 1974, No 7; F. Capelli, *'Réglementation communautaire et réglementation du GATT'*, (réflexions sur les rapports entre le droit communautaire et le droit international), Revue du Marché commun, 1977, pp. 27-43; J. Steenbergen, *'The Status of GATT in Community Law'*, Journal of Trade Law, Vol. 15, No 4, 1981.

This unique situation of an entity having 'succeeded to' States in the exercise of certain responsibilities[1] is further consolidated by the fact that, following the multilateral trade negotiations of 1973-79 (Tokyo Round), the EEC became party – without the additional signature of its Member States – to a whole series of multilateral trade agreements[2] which provided for the establishment, in the form of 'Signatory Committees', of institutions responsible for overseeing the implementation of the agreements' provisions and for helping to settle any disputes which might arise between the parties. The EEC has the *de jure* status of member in these special fringe institutions of GATT whereas it enjoys only a *de facto* equivalent position on the organs of GATT itself.

World Food Council

Article 60 of the rules of procedure of the World Food Council (set up in 1976 under the auspices of the FAO) expressly provides for the European Economic Community (and indeed for Comecon, other intergovernmental organizations having permanent observer status at the United Nations General Assembly and for a number of liberation movements) not only to participate in all the proceedings of the organization likely to be of interest to it but also to put forward 'proposals which may be put to the vote at the request of any member'.

This text is ambiguous (in whose name are the proposals to be tabled? The EEC or its Member States?) and limited in scope (the proposal must be seconded by at least one State). However, it is an advance on the provisions or practices described earlier which often impede the tabling of proposals by observers, in particular the Community.

Section 3: Compatibility of the Communities' status in international organizations and conferences with the requirements of their 'constitution'

Any assessment of the compatibility of the Communities' status, as conferred by international organizations and conferences, with their 'internal constitutional' requirements has, to some extent, to be qualified but is on the whole fairly positive.

1. At their present stage of development and in view of the practice of international organizations and conferences the European Communities will doubtless have to be content with observer status at these institutions for some time to come.

---

[1] As recognized by the Court of Justice of the European Communities in its judgment of 12.12.1972 (Joined Cases 21 to 24/72 *International Fruit* [1972] ECR 1219).

[2] Agreement on governmental procurements; Agreement on the interpretation and application of Articles VI, XVI and XXIII of the General Agreement on Tariffs and Trade (subsidies and countervailing duties); Agreement on the implementation of Article VI of the GATT (dumping); Agreement on import licensing procedures; Agreement and Protocol on the implementation of Article VII of the GATT (value for customs purposes) (Cf. OJ L 71, 1980). For an analysis of these instruments, see in particular: D. Carreau, P. Juillard, Th. Flory, *Droit international économique,* second edition, Paris 1980, p. 298 *et seq.*

On the other hand, they should be able to obtain a number of improvements to this status.

2. For example, the EEC would seem to be in a position to obtain observer status with those few organizations (such as the ICAO) which have not yet granted it that status.

International organizations which have accorded observer status to the EEC on only a fairly tenuous basis (invitation by the secretariat), should have no serious objections to this status being consolidated.

3. It should be possible, through purely practical measures, to obtain a number of improvements to the permanent observer status which the Communities already enjoy with many international organizations.

Such measures should be sufficient to overcome any specific difficulties which the Community representatives may sometimes encounter in gaining access to some negotiating fora or in exercising their right to speak without restriction. The adoption of these measures depends above all on the cohesion and resolve which the Member States of the Communities are able to demonstrate.

4. In view of the present rules and practices in force in international organizations and conferences, it is definitely out of the question for organizations and entities which, like the Communities, enjoy only observer status to be given the right to vote.

In any event, the European Communities could not seek to obtain a right to vote over and above that of their Member States who belong to the organization. Furthermore, if the Communities were to claim a right to vote in their own name, they would doubtless wish to avoid being reduced to a situation in which the number of votes they held was less than the number of their Member States; such a development would be fiercely contested by the latter in any case.

5. If, despite the shortcomings of the status accorded to them, the European Communities actually succeed in various ways and principally via the presidency of the Council of the European Communities, in submitting texts and amendments which reflect their positions, they have achieved their main aim which is to act as a united entity within international organizations and conferences.

The precise legal expression given to this political cohesion may be of only secondary importance as far as non-member countries are concerned.

The Communities may nevertheless wish to obtain legal clarification of the provisions which periodically give rise to discussion as to their representatives' right to take part, without impediment, in formulating the instruments of international organizations and conferences.

Reforms such as these will only be achieved if they are based on initiatives supported by all the Member States and backed by a large number of other delegations.

The European Communities will certainly need time to obtain this support, for they will have to overcome opposition from some quarters and convince many doubters.

Participation of the European Communities in international agreements and other legal instruments

The European Communities' right to be party to international agreements and other commitments has been granted only after negotiations which have sometimes been very difficult. The most critical stage of these problems now appears to be over but, judging by experience, the Communities' participation in instruments of international law established by agreement is still meeting oppostion from non-member countries.

Hitherto, these difficulties have essentially concerned international agreements proper, and above all multilateral agreements. They will be discussed in Chapter I.

The Communities' participation in international commitments embodied in instruments other than agreements, in particular in the decisions and resolutions of international organizations, is still fairly limited. But it does raise a number of questions which deserve consideration and these will be dealt with in Chapter II.

Chapter I – Participation of the European Communities in international agreements

The position as regards participation by the European Communities' in international agreements varies according to whether bilateral or multilateral agreements are involved.

The only requirement for one of the Communities to become party to a bilateral agreement with a non-member country or group of non-member countries is that both parties have agreed to negotiate together and that they have found common ground in respect of the problems to be resolved by the agreement.

The problem is far less straightforward for multilateral agreements. As a general rule, such agreements are open only to participation by States. Consequently, the Communities may not become party to a multilateral agreement unless the States participating in the negotiations give their consent.

In almost every case, the Communities' partners have recognized their (i.e. the Communities') right to participate in multilateral agreements dealing with questions within the Communities' sphere of jurisdiction.

The negotiations to reach this position have often been difficult because of the hostility of a minority of States to the principle of such participation and of the concern of the majority in favour to take elaborate precautions and obtain adequate safeguards.

As a result, even when the principle of participation has been accepted, the Communities' actual participation in these multilateral agreements is almost always subject to more restrictive – or, at the very least more complex – conditions than those governing the participation of States.

This is especially true in respect of: the opening of agreements to participation; acquisition by the Communities of the status of contracting party; their participation in the institutions responsible for the implementation and administration of the agreements.

In the following discussion of these questions it will be apparent, time and again, that the Communities' participation in multilateral agreements creates many more intractable problems when the agreements are to be concluded not only by the Community but also by its Member States ('mixed') agreements) than when they can be concluded by the Community alone ('Community') agreements).

It was therefore thought appropriate to preface this discussion by a number of considerations on the basis and extent of the distinction between the two types of agreement, their respective significance in Community practice and the advantages and disadvantages they may present for the non-member countries concerned.

Section 1: 'Community' agreements and 'mixed' agreements

A – Basis and extent of the distinction

International agreements in which the Communities may be called upon to participate concern, either wholly or in part, matters falling within the jurisdiction conferred upon them by their establishing Treaties.

The principle laid down by these Treaties is, in the first case, that the Community alone is empowered to conclude the proposed agreement. The Member States may not be a party to it even if – as will be seen later[1] – they are bound by the agreement and must adhere to and implement it.

The agreements in this category are commonly referred to by the term already mentioned,[2] i.e. 'Community' agreements.

In the second case, the rule is that Community participation is limited to matters in the agreement which fall within its jurisdiction. The remainder of the agreement may be accepted by the Member States only.

The time-honoured method of settling such cases is the 'mixed' agreement, which is concluded simultaneously by the Community and its Member States.

Express provision to use this method is given only in the Euratom Treaty (Article 103). It is frequently used, however, in the spheres of application of the EEC and ECSC Treaties.[3]

---

[1] See Part Three, p. 126 *et seq.*

[2] See Part One, p. 39.

[3] See R.J. Dupuy, *'La technique de l'accord mixte utilisée par les Communautés européennes',* Annuaire de l'Institut de droit international, 1973, p. 25; *Mixed Agreements,* joint work edited by D. O'Keefe and H.G. Schermers, Kluwer, 1983; see in particular in that publication: C.D. Ehlermann, *'Mixed agreements, a list of problems'* pp. 3-22.

The reason why this practice is commonly adopted stems in part from the fact that some of the agreements negotiated by one or other of the Communities contain provisions which manifestly exceed the limits of their jurisdiction. This is especially true of multilateral agreements.

It seldom occurs in practice that a multilateral agreement negotiated within the framework of an international organization or conference of a universal or regional character relates to matters wholly within the competence of a particular Community. Such an occurrence becomes increasingly unlikely as the negotiating Community is less and less influential in determining the subject matter of the agreement, as the extent of its jurisdiction in the field(s) covered by the agreement becomes more limited than in other sectors and as the range of issues which the agreement is designed to settle becomes wider and more varied.

The Communities' lack of authority to conclude international agreements without the participation of its Member States is far from always being apparent. In the majority of cases, in fact, there is a choice between the 'Community' type of agreement and the 'mixed' agreement and experience has shown that, in such cases, the Member States of the Communities often disagree among themselves or with the Commission on which option to take.

Occasionally, the Commission has referred these differences of view to the Court of Justice[1] for arbitration but this procedure is politically delicate to handle. Furthermore, it is time-consuming and can not be contemplated when the agreement has to be signed quickly. In the majority of cases, the Member States have therefore to settle their differences with the Commission themselves and the compromise often reached has involved a 'mixed' agreement without specific identification of the parts of the agreement which fall, respectively, within either their or the Community's jurisdiction.

In the absence of such identification it is generally difficult to determine, in a given agreement, which provisions predominate, i.e. those relating to subjects in respect of which the Community is competent or those relating to subjects in respect of which the Member States are competent and it would be pointless to attempt to classify these 'mixed' agreements on the basis of that criterion.

What is quite clear, on the other hand, is that whereas the majority of 'mixed' agreements involve the participation of all the Member States alongside the Community, others have been signed and ratified by some of these States only. Examples are the

---

[1] In accordance with the procedure laid down in the second paragraph of Article 228(1) of the EEC Treaty which enables the Commission, and indeed the Council or any Member State, to obtain beforehand the opinion of the Court of Justice as to whether an international agreement envisaged by the EEC is compatible with the provisions of this Treaty. The Commission has invoked this provision on three occasions, namely: in 1975, in connection with an agreement negotiated within the framework of the OECD in respect of export credit, in 1976 concerning a draft agreement with Switzerland on the establishment of a laying-up fund for inland waterway vessels, and in 1978 concerning a draft international natural rubber agreement under the auspices of Unctad. The opinions given by the Court in these three cases were: Opinion 1/75 [1975] ECR 1355, Opinion 1/76 [1977] ECR 741, Opinion 1/78 [1979] ECR 2871.

Paris Convention of 1974 for the prevention of marine pollution from land-based sources,[1] to which neither Luxembourg nor Italy is party and the Barcelona Convention of 1976 for the protection of the Mediterranean Sea against pollution,[2] to which only France and Italy are party. Similarly, the Canberra Convention of 1980 on the Conservation of the Antartic Marine living resources[3] was, as far as the Communities' Member States were concerned, opened for signature only by Belgium, France, the Federal Republic of Germany and the United Kingdom.

The reason for this limited participation was that only a few Member States were liable to be affected by the agreements. Until recently, there were no examples of 'mixed' agreements where particular Member States had refused to participate for reasons of mere expediency. It seemed unlikely that Member States reluctant to sign and ratify an agreement for political reasons would be prepared to allow the Community to participate. Nevertheless such a situation occurred when the Council of the European Communities decided that the EEC should sign the 1982 Convention on the Law of the Sea,[4] although two Member States (the United Kingdom and the Federal Republic of Germany) are not willing to sign it individually.

A further delicate question is whether 'mixed' agreements should be regarded as bilateral or multilateral.[5]

If the essential characteristic of the multilateral agreement is that it establishes relationships in respect of rights and obligations between more than two parties, there is no doubt, in our opinion, that the agreements establishing such relationships, not only between the Community and its Member States and at least two non-member States, but also between these States, are multilateral agreements. This conclusion is not contingent upon whether the Community and its Member States should be considered as constituting a single party or several parties to such agreements.

On the other hand, the question cannot be avoided in the case of agreements which have been concluded by the Community and its Member States with one non-member State only (association agreement between the EEC and Turkey, agreements between the EEC and Algeria, Morocco, Tunisia, etc.) or which – although concluded with several non-member States (e.g. the Lomé Conventions concluded with tens of African, Caribbean and Pacific States ('ACP' States)) – establish relationships in respect of rights and obligations only between the Community and its Member States and each of these

---

[1] See OJ L 194, 1975.

[2] See OJ L 240, 1977. The situation is the same for the protocols to the Barcelona Convention which the EEC subsequently concluded, i.e.: Protocol concerning cooperation, in emergencies, in dealing with pollution of the Mediterranean Sea by oil and other harmful substances (OJ L 162, 1981); Protocol on the protection of the Mediterranean Sea against pollution from land-based sources (OJ L 67, 1983); Protocol on specially-protected areas of the Mediterranean Sea (OJ L 68, 1984).

[3] The text of the convention is given in *Annuaire français de droit international,* 1980, p. 761 *et seq.,* as an annex to the article on this Convention by D. Vignes (pp. 742-761).

[4] The signature of the EEC was given on 7 December 1984.

[5] On this question, see Ph. Allott, *'Adherence to and withdrawal from mixed agreements'* in *Mixed Agreements,* previously-mentioned joint publication, pp. 97-121.

States but not between the latter States themselves. Since the purpose of the 'mixed' agreement is not to establish rights and obligations between the components of the 'European party' to the agreement, i.e. the Community plus Member States, but only to aggregate their powers to enable them to undertake commitments *vis-à-vis* non-member countries over and above those which the Community could undertake alone, it is our opinion that, in the two cases described above, a bilateral agreement – or a set of bilateral agreements – is/are involved in which the Community and its Member States are in fact a single party.[1] Moreover, this opinion appears to be supported by the fact that the above-mentioned agreements have given a joint structure to the institutions they created (EEC-Turkey Association Council, EEC-Algeria Council, ACP-EEC Council of Ministers) and that the decisions they are entitled to take must be adopted unanimously by the 'European party' on the one hand and the contracting non-member country or group of non-member countries on the other.

B – Practice of 'Community' and 'mixed' agreements

1. Multilateral agreements

For the reasons stated earlier, the Community type of agreement has been little used in the negotiation of multilateral agreements.

To date, Community multilateral agreements have been concluded by the EEC only. These are:

(i)   the Geneva Arrangement on international trade in textile products (known as the Multifibre Arrangement of 20.12.1973, renewed, with some changes in 1977 and again in 1981);[2]

(ii) the Tariff Protocol (EEC) and seven of the other multilateral agreements[3] concluded after the multilateral trade negotiations of 1973-79 (Tokyo Round);[4]

(iii) the 1978 Convention on future multilateral cooperation in the North Atlantic fisheries,[5] the 1980 Convention on future multilateral cooperation in the North-East Atlantic fisheries,[6] the 1982 Convention on the conservation of salmon in the

---

[1] Other consequences of this position will be discussed in a later section (pp. 81-82, 86-87).

[2] The text of the 1973 Multifibre Arrangement and its protocol of renewal of 1981 are contained in OJ L 118, 1974 and OJ L 83, 1982 respectively.

[3] The five agreements already mentioned in Part One (p. 53) and the Arrangement concerning beef and veal, the International Arrangement concerning the dairy sector.

[4] All these texts are published in OJ L 71, 1980.

[5] See OJ L 378, 1978. The 1978 Convention replaces the ICNAF Convention of 1949.

[6] See OJ L 227, 1981. The 1980 Convention replaces the NEAFC Convention of 1959.

North Atlantic[1] and the 1982 Convention on fisheries and the conservation of living resources in the Baltic Sea and the Belts;[2,3]

(iv) the international olive oil agreement of 1979;[4]

(v) the 1982 Dublin Agreement on the carriage of passengers by coach or bus.[5]

All the other multilateral agreements concluded to date by the Communities are 'mixed' agreements.

Of the agreements concluded by the EEC (and its Member States) mention will be made of:

(i) two of the multilateral agreements concluded after the multilateral trade negotiations of 1973-79 (Tokyo Round);[6]

(ii) the world commodity agreements, i.e. wheat (and food aid),[7] coffee,[8] cocoa,[9] tin,[10] turalnatural rubber,[11] and jute;[12,13]

(iii) three customs conventions:
- 1973 Kyoto Convention on the simplification and harmonization of customs procedures;[14]
- customs convention on the international transport of goods under cover of TIR carnets (1975 TIR Convention);[15]
- 1982 Geneva Convention on harmonization of goods checks at frontiers;[16]

(iv) a number of environmental protection agreements:
- 1974 Paris Convention (previously mentioned) on the prevention of marine pollution from land-based sources;
- Barcelona Convention and Protocols (previously mentioned) on the protection of the Mediterranean Sea against pollution;

---

[1] OJ L 378, 1982.

[2] OJ L 237, 1983.

[3] It should also be mentioned that the EEC has, by virtue of its sole power in respect of fisheries, 'succeeded to' the rights and obligations previously assumed by Denmark *vis-à-vis* Norway and Sweden under the Trilateral Agreement of 19 December 1966 concerning fishing rights in the Skagerrak and Kattegat. The arrangements to implement this agreement are now negotiated and concluded by the EEC (see, for example, the EEC-Norway/Sweden Agreement of 14.1.1983, OJ L 73, 1983).

[4] See OJ L 327, 1979.

[5] OJ L 230, 1982.

[6] Agreement on technical barriers to trade, Agreement on trade in civil aircraft (OJ L 71, 1980).

[7] 1971 Convention frequently renewed (OJ L 181, 1983).

[8] 1983 Agreement (OJ L 308, 1983).

[9] 1980 Agreement (OJ L 313, 1981).

[10] 1981 Agreement (OJ L 342, 1982).

[11] 1979 Agreement (OJ L 213, 1980).

[12] 1982 Agreement (OJ L 185, 1983).

[13] It should be remembered that the 1980 Geneva Agreement establishing the Common Fund for Commodities, negotiated under the auspices of Unctad (Doc. Unctad TD-IPC-CONF/L 15 of 26.6.1980), is also open to EEC participation.

[14] OJ L 100, 1975.

[15] OJ L 252, 1978.

[16] OJ L 126, 1984.

- 1976 Bonn Agreement on the protection of the Rhine against chemical pollution;[1]
- 1979 Strasbourg Convention (Council of Europe) on the conservation of European wildlife and natural habitats;[2]
- 1979 Bonn Agreement (United Nations) on the conservation of migratory species of wild animals;[3]
- 1979 Geneva Convention on the prevention of long-distance transboundary air pollution;[4]
- Bonn Agreement (1983) for cooperation in dealing with pollution of the North Sea by oil and other harmful substances;[5]
- 1978 Convention (Council of Europe) for the protection of animals kept for farming purposes.[6]

The EEC may also become party (together with four of its Member States) to the 1980 Canberra Convention (already quoted) on the conservation of Antarctic marine living resources.

As far as can be ascertained, the ECSC is not party to any multilateral agreement.[7] The EAEC has been accorded the status of party to only one agreement of the 'mixed' type, i.e.: the 1979 Vienna Convention on the physical protection of nuclear materials.

2. Bilateral agreements

The bilateral agreements concluded by the Communities frequently take the form of 'Community' agreements. This is chiefly because the Communities have often been instrumental in determining the subject of these agreements and have been able to restrict it to matters in respect of which they have full jurisdiction. On the other hand, some bilateral agreements concluded by the Communities have taken the form of 'mixed' agreements.

Although this chapter is devoted principally to an examination of the problems raised by the Communities' participation in these multilateral agreements, the authors thought it would be helpful to list the main bilateral agreements, whether of the 'Community' or 'mixed' type, to which the Communities are party.

---

[1] OJ 240, 1977.

[2] OJ L. 38, 1982.

[3] OJ L 210, 1982.

[4] OJ L 171, 1981.

[5] OJ L 188, 1984.

[6] OJ L 323, 1978.

[7] The 1979 Geneva Protocols (on tariffs) resulting from the multilateral trade negotiations of 1973-79 (Tokyo Round) were, in respect of the products covered by the ECSC Treaty, concluded not by the ECSC itself but by its Member States (Decision of 10.12.1979 of the representatives of the governments of the Member States of the ECSC meeting within the Council of the European Communities, OJ L 71, 1980). Strictly speaking, therefore, these are not ECSC agreements.

Agreements concluded by the EEC

First, the trade agreements (or commercial cooperation agreements) concluded with:

(i)   the member countries of the European Free Trade Association (EFTA), i.e.: Austria,[1] Finland,[2] Iceland,[3] Norway,[4] Portugal,[3] Sweden,[4] Switzerland[5] and two other European countries, Spain[6] and Romania;[7]

(ii)   Israel;[8]

(iii) Canada;[9]

(iv)   Argentina,[10] Brazil,[11] Mexico[12] and Uruguay,[13] 'Cartagena Agreement' (or Andean Pact) and its Member States: Bolivia, Colombia, Ecuador, Peru, Venezuela;[14]

(v)   China;[15]

(vi)   India,[16] Pakistan, [17] Bangladesh,[18] Sri Lanka;[19]

(vii) the member countries of Asean: Indonesia, Malaysia, Philippines, Singapore, Thailand, Brunei-Darussalam;[20]

(viii) the Yemen Arab Republic.[21]

Mention should also be made of the many bilateral agreements concluded by the EEC concerning trade in specific products, for example:

---

[1]   Agreement of 22.7.1972 (OJ L 300, 1972).
[2]   Agreement of 5.10.1973 (OJ L 328, 1973).
[3]   Agreement of 22.7.1972 (OJ L 301, 1972).
[4]   Agreement of 14.5.1973 (OJ L 171, 1973).
[5]   Agreement of 22.7.1972 (OJ L 300, 1972). The EEC-Switzerland agreement also applies to the Principality of Liechtenstein.
[6]   Agreement of 29.6.1970 (OJ L 182, 1972).
[7]   Agreement of 28.7.1980 on trade in industrial products and agreement of the same date setting up the Joint Committee (OJ L 352, 1980).
[8]   Agreement of 11.5.1975 (OJ L 136, 1975). This Agreement was supplemented by additional protocols and by protocols on financial cooperation concluded simultaneously by the EEC and by its Member States (see OJ L 270, 1978 and OJ L 335, 1983).
[9]   Framework agreement of 6.7.1976 (OJ L 260, 1976).
[10] Agreement of 8.11.1971 (OJ L 249, 1971).
[11] Agreement of 18.9.1980 (OJ L 281, 1982).
[12] Agreement of 15.7.1975 (OJ L 247, 1975).
[13] Agreement of 2.4.1973 (OJ L 333, 1973).
[14] Agreement of 17.12.1983 (OJ L 153, 1984).
[15] Agreement of 3.4.1978 (OJ L 123, 1978).
[16] Agreement of 23.6.1981 (OJ L 328, 1981).
[17] Agreement of 1.6.1976 (OJ L 168, 1976).
[18] Agreement of 19.10.1976 (OJ L 319, 1976).
[19] Agreement of 22.7.1975 (OJ L 247, 1975).
[20] Agreement of 7.3.1980 (OJ L 144, 1980) and protocol of 15.11.1984 (OJ L 81, 1985).
[21] Agreement of 29.1.1985 (OJ L 26, 1985).

(i)   textiles (bilateral agreements concluded under the Multifibre Arrangement of 1973, which was renewed in 1977 and again in 1981;[1]

(ii) sheep– and goatmeat,[2] wine[3] and manioc.[4,5]

The EEC has also concluded a large number of bilateral fisheries agreements with non-member countries: Spain,[6] Norway,[7] Sweden,[7] Finland,[8] United States,[9] Canada,[10] Senegal,[11] Guinea-Bissau,[12] Guinea (Conakry),[13] Equatorial Guinea,[14] Sao Tome Principe[15] and Seychelles.[16]

Mention will also be made of bilateral agreements concluded by the EEC on various subjects such as information,[17] scientific and technical research[18] and humanitarian aid.[19]

Agreements concluded by the ECSC

Reference will be made chiefly to the 'voluntary limitation' agreements which the main countries supplying iron and steel products have concluded with the ECSC every year since 1978.[20] Mention should also be made of the 1982 Arrangement by which the

---

[1] By the end of 1982, 26 bilateral agreements had been concluded, covering the period 1983-86. Under the Multifibre Arrangement: see OJ L 374, 1982 for the text of the regulation of the Council of the European Communities implementing these agreements.

[2] See in particular the agreements concluded by the EEC with Argentina (OJ L 275, 1980), Australia (OJ L 275, 1980) Bulgaria (OJ L 43, 1982), Hungary (OJ L 150, 1981), New Zealand (OJ L 257, 1980), Poland (OJ L 137, 1981), Czechoslovakia (OJ L 204, 1982) and Uruguay (OJ L 275, 1980).

[3] See in particular the EEC-Austria Agreement on quality wines (OJ L 389, 1981).

[4] See the EEC-Thailand, EEC-Indonesia, EEC-Brazil agreements (OJ L 219, 1982).

[5] Mention should also be made of the numerous agreements concluded by the EEC within GATT on 'deconsolidation' and on rules for trade in natural and processed agricultural products (cheese, in particular).

[6] OJ L 332, 1980.

[7] OJ L 226, 1980.

[8] OJ L 192, 1983.

[9] OJ L 141, 1977 and L 272, 1984.

[10] OJ L 379, 1981.

[11] OJ L 154, 1979 and L 226, 1980.

[12] OJ L 226, 1980 and L 84, 1983.

[13] OJ L 111, 1983.

[14] OJ L 237, 1983.

[15] OJ L 282, 1983.

[16] OJ L 79, 1984.

[17] For example: EEC-Switzerland (OJ L 214, 1979), EEC-Sweden (OJ L 174, 1982) and EEC-Finland (OJ L 345, 1982) agreements on the interconnection of the Community data transmission network ('Euronet') to the networks of those three countries.

[18] For example: EEC-Sweden agreement on a European timber research and development programme (OJ L 185, 1983).

[19] Example: Convention concluded for the period 1984-86 between the EEC and the United Nations Relief and Works Agency for Palestinian Refugees (UNRWA) regarding help provided for refugees in countries of the Middle East (OJ L 188, 1984).

[20] In 1984, there were arrangements of this type between the ECSC and 15 countries (not published in the Official Journal).

ECSC (and the EEC for products not covered by the ECSC Treaty) undertook to limit their exports of certain iron and steel products to the United States from 1 November 1982 to 31 December 1985 inclusive.[1,2]

Agreements concluded by the EAEC (Euratom)

Mention should be made of the various cooperation agreements linking the EAEC with the United States[3] and Canada,[4] the 1981 agreement with Australia on the transfer of nuclear materials[5] and the EAEC-Switzerland,[6] EAEC-Sweden[7] and EAEC-Spain[8] agreements in the fields of thermonuclear fusion and plasma physics.

'Mixed' bilateral agreements

Important 'mixed' agreements have been concluded by the EEC. They are either association or cooperation agreements with:

(i)   the countries of the Mediterranean basin, i.e.: Turkey,[9] Cyprus,[10] Malta,[11] Yugoslavia,[12] Algeria,[13] Morocco,[14] Tunisia,[15] Egypt,[16] Lebanon,[17] Syria,[18] Jordan;[19]

(ii) African, Caribbean and Pacific (ACP) countries, i.e. the countries of the Lomé Convention.[20]

In addition to a section on trade most of the agreements contain provisions relating to financial cooperation, industrial, scientific, technical and agricultural cooperation, the

---

[1] OJ L 307, 1982 and L 215, 1983.

[2] The trade and economic cooperation framework agreement with Canada was concluded by the ECSC as well as the EEC (see p. 64 above) and the EAEC (see note 4 thereafter).

[3] OJ 17, 1959; 31, 1961; 72, 1962; 163, 1964 and L 139, 1974.

[4] OJ 60, 1959; L 65, 1978; L 27, 1982. Note also that the commercial and economic cooperation framework agreement with Canada was concluded not only by the EEC (see above, p. 64) and the ECSC (see note 2 above), but also by the EAEC (OJ L 260, 1976).

[5] OJ L 281, 1982.

[6] OJ L 242, 1978 and L 116, 1982.

[7] OJ L 162, 1976 and L 116, 1982.

[8] OJ L 238, 1983.

[9] Association agreement of 12.9.1963 and Additional Protocol of 23.11.1970 (OJ L 217, 1964 and 293, 1972).

[10] Association agreement of 19.12.1972 (OJ L 133, 1973).

[11] Association agreement of 5.12.1970, (OJ L 61, 1971).

[12] Cooperation agreement of 2.4.1980 (OJ L 41, 1983).

[13] Cooperation agreement of 26.4.1976 (OJ 263, 1978).

[14] Cooperation agreement of 27.4.1976 (OJ 264, 1978).

[15] Cooperation agreement of 25.4.1976 (OJ L 265, 1978).

[16] Cooperation agreement of 18.1.1977 (OJ L 266, 1978).

[17] Cooperation agreement of 3.5.1977 (OJ L 267, 1978).

[18] Cooperation agreement of 18.1.1977 (OJ L 269, 1978).

[19] Cooperation agreement of 18.1.1977 (OJ L 268, 1978).

[20] Lomé II Convention signed on 31.10.1979 by 58 ACP States (OJ L 347, 1980). Six new States acceded to the Convention after its signature, i.e.: Saint Vincent and the Grenadines, Vanuatu, Zimbabwe, Belize, Antigua and Barbuda, St Kitts and Nevis; consequently, there are now 64 ACP States which are party to the Convention with the EEC and its Member States. Lomé III Convention (not yet in force) was signed on 8.12.1984 by those 64 States and by Mozambique.

right of establishment, labour, etc. The Member States of the European Community considered that the EEC was not competent to undertake negotiations in its own right in these various fields.[1] Consequently, a 'mixed' agreement formula was used to conclude the above agreements.

The EAEC (Euratom) is also party to 'mixed' bilateral agreements. Particular mention should be made of the Verification Agreement concerning Euratom safeguards concluded in 1973[2] under the Treaty on the Non-proliferation of Nuclear Weapons between, on the one hand, the EAEC and those of its Member States which do not possess such weapons and the International Atomic Energy Agency (IAEA) on the other.

The bilateral agreements concluded under the aegis of the ECSC are rather special. Firstly, they merely supplement, in respect of the products or fields covered by the ECSC Treaty, trade or commercial cooperation agreements concluded by the EEC (alone) or the commercial sections of association of cooperation agreements concluded by the EEC (alone) or the commercial sections of association or cooperation agreements concluded by the EEC and its Member States. Secondly, some of these agreements have been concluded simultaneously by the ECSC and its Member States;[3] others have been concluded by the ECSC Member States acting together but without the participation of the ECSC itself.[4] Strictly speaking, therefore, the latter are not Community agreements.

C – Advantages and disadvantages for non-member countries of the 'Community' agreement and the 'mixed' agreement

In each case, the choice to be made between the 'Community' agreement and the 'mixed' agreement depends solely on the extent of the powers vested in the Communites by the establishing Treaties. The way in which the relevant provisions of these Treaties are interpreted – frequently involving a considerable degree of latitude – is the sole responsibility of the institutions of the Communities and their Member States. Non-member countries have no say in this exercise.

---

[1] This position is based on a restrictive interpretation, not supported by the Commission, of the powers which the EEC enjoys pursuant to Article 238 of the EEC Treaty ('The Community may conclude with a third State ... agreements establishing an association involving reciprocal rights and obligations, common action and special procedures ...').

[2] Brussels Agreement of 5.4.1973 (OJ L 51, 1978).

[3] For example: agreements concluded by the ECSC and its Member States with: Austria, Portugal, Sweden (OJ L 350, 1973), Finland, Norway (OJ L 348, 1974), Yugoslavia (OJ L 41, 1983); ECSC protocols to the commercial and economic cooperation agreements with Canada (OJ L 260, 1976) and India (OJ L 352, 1981).

[4] For example: agreements concluded by the ECSC Member States with: Turkey (OJ L 293, 1972), Iceland, Switzerland (OJ L 350, 1973), Israel (OJ L 165, 1975), Algeria (OJ L 263, 1978), Tunisia (OJ L 265, 1978), Morocco (OJ L 234, 1978), Egypt, Lebanon, Jordan, Syria (OJ L 316, 1979) and the ACP States party to the Lomé Convention (OJ L 347, 1980).

In practice, few countries attempt to influence the decisions made by the Communities and their Member States. Yet the non-member countries cannot remain indifferent. In reality, the 'Community' agreement and the 'mixed' agreement may well have differing political and legal repercussions for these.

1. Political aspect

The 'Community' agreement, especially the bilateral type, undoubtedly involves a greater degree of political recognition by the contracting non-member country or countries of the identity and specific powers of the Communities than is the case with a 'mixed' agreement where the communities are only supported and backed up by their Member States.

This applies in particular to the negotiations – now at a standstill – which the EEC conducted over several years (1976-80) with the Council for Mutual Economic Assistance (CMEA) and the Member States of that organization.

It emerged clearly from these negotiations that the Community's opposite numbers wanted to normalize their relations with the Community by means of an agreement but were not prepared fully to recognize the Community, its aims and powers, and institutional rules and practices. It was undoubtedly this unwillingness which led them to keep reiterating the wish – not shared by the Community – that the individual Member States of the Community should accede to any agreement.

A particular State's preference for the 'mixed' agreement formula may have nothing whatsoever to do with its reluctance to grant full recognition to the Community.

Many States are still unused to dealing with the Community and often have little knowledge of its structure and responsibilities. On the other hand, many have a long-standing and special relationship with the Member States of the Community and the 'mixed' agreement formula may appear attractive to the extent it helps foster a direct dialogue with those States. Experience has shown that the governments of the Member States of the Community have always taken this attitude into account when choosing between a 'Community' agreement and a 'mixed' agreement.

2. Legal aspect

Countries wishing to conclude an agreement with the Community may also have legal reasons for preferring one or other of the two formulae.

Since, in general, there is no requirement under a 'mixed' agreement to provide specific information to the contracting country or countries on which areas of the agreement come under Community jurisdiction and which come under the Member States' jurisdiction, such an agreement may be regarded as involving a concurrent commitment for both the Community and its Member States in respect of each of the obligations devolving upon the European party. This particular feature of the 'mixed' agreement may offer advantages for the Community's partners, especially in the event of a dispute. This point will be discussed further in Part Three (see pp. 132 and 150).

It would appear, however, that the confusion created by the 'mixed' agreement as regards determination of the commitments and responsibilities entered into respectively by the Community and its Member States often causes concern for the non-member countries. What is striking is the insistence shown by many of these countries during the negotiations in demanding more precise information on how these responsibilities and commitments are to be allocated and in seeking an assurance that the dual participation of the Community and its Member States will not give them voting rights in the institutions set up by the agreements over and above those which would have been granted to the Member States, if the Community had not been a party to the agreements.

From the legal standpoint, the non-member countries do not appear to gain any more marked benefit from a 'mixed' agreement than they would from a 'Community' agreement.[1]

Section 2: The Communities' right to be party to international agreements

A – Recognition of this right by non-member countries

The Communities' right to be party to international agreements is now recognized by the great majority of States.

This situation has come about because growing numbers of States have felt obliged either to conclude bilateral agreements with the Communities on an individual basis or to give their collective support to requests from the Communities to participate in multilateral agreements.

Getting this support is not always easy for the Communities, particularly when a very large number of States have to be convinced that there are good grounds for a request to participate in an agreement. This is especially true of the multilateral agreements negotiated under the auspices of international organizations of a universal character such as the United Nations, its subsidiary organs and its specialized agencies.

Many States do not always see clearly the need for the Community to become party to a multilateral agreement especially when such participation is in addition to that of its Member States.

---

[1] Especially as, under the EEC's own 'constitution' (Article 228 of the EEC Treaty), EEC agreements are 'binding upon the Member States'. This point will be considered again in Part Three, p. 126.

Furthermore, the Community's requests for participation sometimes come up against tactical objections from the other parties, fearing that the Community's participation might further complicate already very difficult negotiations and delay their outcome.

In practice, the Communities have always been able to overcome these difficulties since at least their own Member States have been in favour and the non-member States involved have not in principle been opposed to recognition and affirmation of the Communities' identity and international powers.

A number of precedents have been set over the years and experience has shown that no State has ever refused to give the Community the kind of support which it had given on previous occasions.

B – Opposition from Eastern European countries

By contrast, the Communities' participation in international agreements has always met with hostility from the Soviet Union and its Comecon (CMEA) and Warsaw Pact allies. As already stated,[1] these countries have so far refused all official recognition of the Communities.[2]

Accordingly, the USSR and its allies have, on almost every occasion, attempted to block the Community's requests to participate in multilateral agreements.

On rare occasions, where the small number of parties to the agreements has meant that these countries were in a strong position, this attempt has succeeded. For example, the USSR and certain other Eastern European countries were able to block the EEC's application to accede to the Convention on the protection of the marine environment of the Baltic Sea area.

In all other cases, support from a majority of States has enabled the Community to overcome the opposition from these countries.

Finding themselves unable to oppose the actual principle of Community participation in multilateral agreements, these same countries have frequently tried to restrict the political and legal scope of the Community's participation.

---

[1] See Part One, pp. 20 and 21.

[2] Even though some of these States have in fact concluded agreements or arrangements with the EEC (EEC-Romania agreements of 1980, already quoted) EEC-Bulgaria and EEC-Poland agreements on trade in textile products (OJ L 330, 1982 and OJ L 107, 1982 respectively), EEC agreements with Bulgaria, Hungary, Poland, Czechoslovakia, already referred to, on trade in sheep – and goatmeat and agreements with the ECSC (Bulgaria, Hungary, Poland, Romania and Czechoslovakia are among the countries which are party to the voluntary restraint arrangements concerning exports of certain steel products to the ECSC, referred to on p. 65, note 20).

In 1979, for example the USSR proposed that the text presented by the EEC to the Third United Nations Conference on the Law of the Sea with a view to being accepted as a contracting party to the convention drawn up by this Conference, be replaced by a provision under which the EEC would have been allowed only to deposit a unilateral declaration committing itself to acceptance of the rights and obligations laid down by the Convention. This counter-proposal was rejected by the EEC and most of the States participating in the Conference.

Where they are unable to block the inclusion in a multilateral agreement of a clause enabling the Community to become a contracting party on an equal footing with the other States, the USSR and the other Eastern European countries generally issue a unilateral declaration when the agreement is being negotiated and signed or when the instruments of ratification are deposited, to the effect that their participation in the Treaty in no way affects their position *vis-à-vis* certain international organizations'.[1] This means that their participation will not result in any official recognition of the Community.

On several occasions, the USSR and other Eastern European countries have gone even further by issuing a unilateral declaration stating that the fact that the Community is party to the same multilateral agreement as they are themselves will not involve them in any legal obligation *vis-à-vis* the Community.

The Community has objected to these declarations whenever the multilateral agreement giving rise to the delcaration has clearly prohibited the parties to the agreement from entering a reservation on the provision relating to the Community's participation. In each case, the Community's objection has been notified to the depositary of the agreement through the offices of the President of the Council of the European Communities, acting on behalf of both the Community and its Member States.

It should be noted that the above-mentioned declarations have been issued only in respect of those multilateral agrrements to be concluded under the 'mixed' agreement formula. The USSR and its allies have never run the risk of issuing such a declaration in respect of multilateral agreements to be concluded as 'Community' agreements, as they would then have been denying that approval of the agreements in question by the Council of the European Communities, i.e. by an institution composed of representatives of its Member States, had any legal significance.

C – Other difficulties

The Communities' participation in international agreements may sometimes be thwarted by obstacles even more difficult to overcome than those already mentioned.

---

[1] A declaration of this kind was issued, for example, when the USSR and the German Democratic Republic signed the 1978 Convention on future multilateral cooperation in North-Atlantic fisheries (see p. 61 above).

One example is where the Communities wish to become party to a multilateral agreement already signed or implemented, to which only States have been allowed to accede.

Post hoc amendments to the provisions of such an agreement are therefore required if it is to be opened to the Communities.

Such an operation may take considerable time, particularly if there is no simplified revision procedure to invoke and if a large number of States have to agree to the changes being made. Furthermore, the Community's need to amend the agreement means that its position as an applicant is even more awkward that it would be if it were seeking the inclusion of a clause allowing participation in an agreement still in process of negotiation. In the latter case, acceptance of the Community's request may be expedited by the wish of the States participating in the negotiations to settle this and other matters as soon as possible in order to bring the discussions to a close. Obviously, this cannot happen when the amendment of an isolated point in an agreement already adopted is involved.

In view of these difficulties, the Community has often thought it better to refrain from seeking the right to accede to existing agreements. The circumstances in which the opposite line has been taken relate to agreements to which there were only a few signatory States, most of whom belonged to the Community. Noteworthy cases, however, are the Council of Europe convention of 1968 for the protection of animals during international transport and the Berne Agreement of 1963 setting up the International Commission for the protection of the Rhine against pollution. In both cases, EEC participation was made possible by the adoption of a special accession protocol by the parties to these agreements.[1]

Mention should also be made of the important Commission proposal,[2] approved by the European Parliament[3] in favour of the Communities' accession to the 1950 European Convention for the protection of human rights and fundamental freedoms.[4]

The second case deserving of mention is that of the international conventions negotiated and adopted under the auspices of the International Labour Organization. This organization has a 'constitution' which lays down, through general provisions, all the conditions and procedures applicable to the conclusion and implementation of the con-

---

[1] The protocol providing for EEC accession to the Convention for the protection of animals during international transport was opened for signature by the Member States of the Council of Europe on 10.5.1979. It will enter into force once all the parties to the convention have ratified it; in the meantime, the EEC is applying the provisions of the Convention on an independent basis (see Directive 77/489 of 18.7.1977, OJ L 22, 1977). Under an additional agreement, the EEC became a member of the International Commission for the protection of the Rhine against pollution (Bonn, 3.12.1976: text in OJ L 240, 1977).

[2] Document COM(79) 210 final of 2.5.1979.

[3] Opinion published in OJ C 304, 1982.

[4] See N. Brown and J. MacBride, *'Observations on the proposed accession by the European Community to the European Convention on Human Rights',* American Journal of Comparative Law, Vol XXIX, No 4, 1981, pp. 691-705; G.Cohen-Jonathan, *'La problématique de l'adhésion des Communautés Européennes à la Convention européenne des droits de l'homme',* Mélanges en l'honneur de P.H. Teitgen, Pedone, Paris, 1984, pp. 81-108.

ventions drawn up by the organization. Moreover, these general provisions[1] do not allow entities other than States to become party to such conventions.

The EEC came up against these provisions in connection with an ILO Convention dealing with matters within its sphere of competence.[2] At the request of the Commission of the European Communities and also of some of the employers' and trade union organizations represented in the ILO, the International Labour Office considered the question of the participation of regional organizations in ILO conventions and concluded that the ILO constitution did in fact preclude such participation.[3] The International Labour Office did, however, contemplate acceptance of the idea that the deposit by the EEC of an instrument of acceptance of a convention drawn up by the organization should be regarded as equivalent to the ratification of that convention by all the Member States of the Community.

This compromise has received a mixed welcome – very favourable, at least from a practical point of view, in certain Community circles but rather unfavourable, one suspects, in countries such as the USSR.

Section 3: Terms on which the European Communities can participate in international agreements

In certain cases, the Community is allowed to participate in an international agreement on exactly the same terms and conditions as the States, so that no special clause concerning the Community has to be incorporated in the text of the agreement.

This has so far been the case with all bilateral agreements. It is also true of certain multilateral agreements, for which it was agreed from the outset that the Community would be entitled to participate on exactly the same footing as the other parties.

For the moment, this is so for a few agreements only. They include the 1976 Bonn agreement (previously mentioned) on the protection of the Rhine against chemical pollution, the 1978 and 1980 conventions (previously mentioned) on future multilateral cooperation in the North and North-East Atlantic Fisheries and the 1982 Dublin agreement (previously mentioned) on the carriage of passengers by road, by coach and bus.

Apart from these special cases, the attribution to the Community of the right to become a contracting party to a multilateral agreement is always subject to special clauses included in the agreement.

---

[1] In particular, Article 19.5 of the ILO constitution.
[2] Convention No 153 concerning hours of work and rest periods in road transport.
[3] See ILO document quoted earlier: GB. 215/SC/4/1 of February-March 1981.

Such clauses formulate, in appropriate legal terms, the political agreement reached between the States participating in the negotiations, as regards the principles and terms of Community participation in the agreement.

In particular, the basis on which the agreement will be opened to such participation has to be established. In most cases, this raises two separate questions in practice.

The first, which may be surprising at first sight, is whether the clause to be incorporated in the agreement should refer to the Community by name or should be addressed, anonymously, to a category of organizations of entities, in which the Community might be included.

The second question is whether the agreement will be opened for signature by the Community or whether it will only offer it the opportunity to accede later.

A – Formulation of the Community participation clause

It is generally when recognition of the Community's right to become a contracting party to a multilateral agreement has appeared to be automatic, or has not given rise to any special political difficulties, that the clause embodied in the agreement refers expressly to the EEC (or the ECSC where appropriate).

In such cases the formula used is for example as follows: 'This agreement will be open for acceptance by the European Economic Community by signature or otherwise. 'This is the form of words used in the most recent agreements negotiated under the auspices of GATT: arrangement for international trade in textiles (Multifibre Arrangement of 1973, extended in 1977 and again in 1981), agreements resulting from multilateral trade negotiations from 1973 to 1979 (Tokyo Round) (already quoted).

Identical forms of words are found in the previously-mentioned 1974 Paris Convention on the prevention of marine pollution from land-based sources and in a number of conventions worked out in the Council of Europe.

Using a different form of words, participation clauses referring explicitly to the EEC have also been included in certain world commodity agreements (1971 International wheat trade convention, 1977 International sugar agreement).[1]

---

[1] The clause in the wheat trade convention is exactly the same as that in the sugar agreement (to which the EEC did not ultimately become party) and reads: 'Any reference to "the government" or "governments" in the present protocol shall be deemed to apply also to the European Economic Community (hereinafter referred to as "the Community"). In consequence, any reference in the present protocol to "signature" or "the deposit of instruments of ratification, acceptance, approval or conclusion" or to "an instrument of accession" or "a declaration of provisional application" by a government shall, in the case of the Community, be deemed to apply also for signature or declaration of provisional application on behalf of the Community by its competent authority and for deposit of the instrument required by the institutional procedures of the Community for the conclusion of an international agreement'.

A number of multilateral agreements have granted the right to participate not only to the EEC but also to 'similar' or 'comparable' organizations.

This extension of the participation clause has in most cases been deprived of any real significance because there are no organizations similar or comparable to the EEC. The sole purpose has been to give the visible impression that the Community was not being given special privileges for itself alone.

The Community has never objected in any way to this practice. It has, on the contrary, seen it as an easier way of obtaining the participation clause it was seeking.

The principal agreements which contain provisions referring to both the EEC and any 'similar' or 'comparable' organizations are: the 1976 Barcelona Convention on the protection of the Mediterranean Sea against pollution, the international olive oil (1979), rubber (1979), cocoa (1980), tin (1981) and coffee (1983) agreements.[1]

In a number of multilateral agreements, the participation clause does not refer to the Community specifically but to a category of organizations or entities in which it may be included.

In most cases, the purpose of this 'anonymous' formula has been to give satisfaction to the USSR and the other East European countries. When they are unable to oppose the actual principle of Community participation in multilateral agreements to which they themselves intend to become parties, these countries try at least to prevent such agreements from making direct reference to an international organization which they do not recognize. This they can do by means of the 'anonymous' formula.

Widely differing periphrases have been used to refer to the Communities without naming them'

(i) 'customs and economic unions';[2]

(ii) 'organizations for regional economic integration set up by sovereign States with powers to negotiate, conclude and apply international agreements on subjects covered by the present convention';[3]

(iii) 'international organizations and regional organizations of an integrating or other character, provided that each such organization be set up by sovereign States and has powers to negotiate, conclude and apply international agreements relating to areas covered by the present convention';[4]

---

[1] Previously mentioned.

[2] Previously-mentioned 1973 Kyoto convention, Article 11; previously-mentioned TIR agreement of 1975, Article 52.3.

[3] Above-mentioned 1979 Convention on the prevention of long-distance transboundary air pollution, Article 14; above-mentioned Bonn Agreement (1979) on the conservation of migratory species of wild animals, Article 1, K); previously-mentioned Geneva Convention (1982), Article 16.1.

[4] Previously-mentioned Vienna Convention (1979) on the physical protection of nuclear materials, Article 18, 4 (a).

(iv) 'organizations for regional economic integration set up by sovereign States, to which the Member States of the organization have transferred full or partial powers in the areas to which the present convention applies';[1]

(v) 'intergovernmental organization set up by States which have transferred to it powers in matters covered by the convention, including powers to conclude treaties on such subjects'.[2]

In most of the above cases, the form of words used can refer only to the Community. In other cases it may effectively apply to other organizations.

This would appear to be the case with the clause incorporated in the Convention on the Law of the Sea. The EEC itself suggested in 1976 and again in 1979 that an 'anonymous' clause be included in the draft convention, to allow for the possibility that an organization such as the Cartagena Agreement (or Andean Pact) might participate in the agreement. Experience has shown, that in cases of this kind, the use of a form of words which could apply to organizations other than the Community might gain allies for the Community.

Two further comments are called for on the 'anonymous' participation clause.

Firstly, it may create doubts as to the effective inclusion of the Community in the abstract category of organizations or entities which it defines. To remove all ambiguity, the Community has sometimes found it necessary to make a unilateral declaration to the effect that it considered itself to be duly included in the category adopted. For example, the Community representative made such a declaration when the United Nations Economic Commission for Europe adopted the aforementioned 1979 convention on long-distance transboundary air pollution. This declaration by the Community raised no objection from the USSR and the other Eastern European countries, which had however only accepted the principle of Community participation in the convention after protracted and difficult negotiations.

Secondly, the 'anonymous' clauses have sometimes been framed in such a way as to open the agreement to some clearly determined organizations or entities but not to others.

For example, the form of words used in the convention on long-distance transboundary air pollution ('organizations for regional economic integration set up by sovereign

---

[1] Aforementioned 1980 Canberra Convention on the conservation of the marine flora and fauna in the Antarctic, Article XXIX, 2.

[2] 1982 Convention on the Law of the Sea, drafted by the Third United Nations Conference of the Law of the Sea, (1973-82), Article 305.1, (f) and Annex IX, Article 1. The full French text of the convention and its annexes is reproduced in *Notes et Études documentaires,* No 4703-4704, 28.1.1983, *La Documentation française,* Paris. The English text is reproduced in *International Legal Materials,* Vol. XXI, No 6 (November 1982), p. 1261 *et. seq.*

States . . .') undoubtedly has the effect of excluding even the possibility of participation by the Council for Mutual Economic Assistance (Comecon). Similarly, the emphasis laid in the clause in the Convention on the Law of the Sea on the fact that organizations entitled to become contracting parties to that convention must have been set up by States, exclude even the possibility of participation by entities such as liberation movements.[1]

B – Signature or accession

Under the terms of Article 11 of the 1969 Vienna Convention on the Law of Treaties: 'The consent of a State to be bound by a treaty can be expressed by signature, the exchange of instruments constituting a treaty, ratification, acceptance, approval or by any other agreed method'.[2]

The consent of the Communities to be bound by agreements entered into with States is expressed, in practice, by the same methods (except ratification proper)[3] as those enumerated in Article 11 of the Vienna Convention.

The Communities can, however, only use these various methods provided the agreement to which they intend to become party does not prohibit them from using one or other such method.

This point is raised because several attempts have been made to prevent the Community from participating, on an equal footing with States, in the signatures of certain agreements and to offer it only the possibility of acceding.

These attempts came to nothing except in one case, namely the previously mentioned Canberra Convention of 1980 on conservation of the marine flora and fauna in the Antarctic, to which the EEC was accorded only the right to accede.[4]

The reasons for this exception from what hitherto seemed to be established practice seem to have been purely political.

---

[1] The liberation movements which took part in the Third United Nations Conference on the Law of the Sea were empowered only to sign the Conference Final Act in their capacity as observers (see Conference Final Act, Annex I, Resolution IV).

[2] These provisions refer only to treaties between States but the 'draft articles' drafted by the International Law Commission concerning treaties between States and international organizations or between two or more international organizations (see Part Three, p. 99) stipulate, for such treaties, provisions similar to those of Article 11 of the Vienna Convention. The Commission proposed, however, that for such treaties (Article 11.2 of the draft) the concept of 'ratification' should not be retained and should be replaced by that of 'act of formal confirmation'. The 1982 Convention on the Law of the Sea (Annex IX, Arts 3, 4 and 5) uses this new terminology with reference to the participation of international organizations (including the EEC).

[3] See note 2 above.

[4] See Article XXIX.2 of the convention.

It is established that when an agreement relates to matters for which powers are shared between the Community and its Member States, acceptance of all its provisions is subject to the jointly-expressed consent of the Community and its Member States.

In accordance with this rule, practice has for a long time been moving towards the simultaneous deposit of acceptance instruments by the Community and its Member States, so that the agreement can enter into force for them on the same date.

The fact that States and in particular Member States of the Community are authorized to sign, over a given period of time, an agreement to which the Community will only be entitled to accede later, is not, properly speaking, such as to threaten the above-mentioned Community rules and practices. It may, however, deprive the Community and its Member States of free choice of the time which they deem appropriate for the simultaneous deposit of their instruments of acceptance. This could be the case if the Community and its Member States considered that they should complete this formality very quickly, that is before the expiry date of the period concerned.

The Member States could express their consent to be bound by the agreement before the expiry date of the period concerned by, for example, signing without any reservation clause of ratification. The Community could not do this. The simultaneous deposit of instruments of acceptance by the Community and its Member States could, therefore, not take place until after the time limit set for the States to sign the agreement.

This case is obviously highly theoretical. Firstly, it is not very frequent for States to sign agreements without the 'subject to ratification' clause or to be in a position to sign very quickly. Secondly, many agreements stipulate signature subject to ratification and in such cases States are free to choose the time for expressing their final consent to being bound by the agreement. Lastly, the rule of Community law which requires the simultaneous deposit of instruments of acceptance by the Community and its Member States applies only to agreements already in force or which would be brought into force by such deposit. This is not usually the case with a multilateral agreement just opened for signature.

The restriction whereby the Community can only accede subsequently to an agreement open for signature by States only seems hardly likely, therefore, to have any real consequences.

It should be noted further that treaty law does not distinguish, as regards legal effects, between (a) consent expressed by a signature, whether or not followed by ratification, (b) acceptance or approval, and (c) consent expressed by accession.

The foregoing arguments show that the considerations which led the States participating in the negotiations for the 1980 Canberra Convention to allow the EEC only the right to accede had no legal substance or practical effects.

Section 4: Ways in which the Communities can acquire the status of a contracting party to an international agreement

Article 2(g) of the 1969 Vienna Convention on the Law of Treaties provides that a State becomes party to a treaty when it has consented to be bound by that treaty and when the latter actually comes into force.

In the previously-mentioned 'draft articles' for treaties between States and international organizations or between two or more international organizations, the International Law Commission expressed the opinion that the rule in Article 2(g) should be purely and simply extended to international organizations.

In our view, the positions so taken by the International Law Commission in no way prejudges the terms on which an international organization such as the Community can acquire the status of a contracting party to an international agreement.

Does this mean that the consent of an international organization to be bound by an agreement and the entry into force of that agreement as regards itself could be subjected to any conditions whatsoever, over and above those which apply to States in the matter and, in particular, that those conditions need take no account of the organization's own rules?

The answer to this question must be 'No'. Treaty law in fact admits that certain rules of the internal law of States and international organizations must be respected, as otherwise their consent to be bound by international agreements could be completely valueless.

It is against this background that consideration will now be given to the validity in international law of obligations which have been imposed on the Communities in a number of cases, as a condition for their right to become party to an international agreement.

Special consideration will be given to the case of international agreements which have subordinated the right of the Communities to declare their consent to be bound either to the condition that all their Member States, or at least the majority of them, have expressed their consent or to the condition that the Communities attach to the notification or deposit of their instrument of acceptance a declaration specifying the parts of the agreement in respect of which they have powers or to both conditions simultaneously.

A – *Compulsory joint participation by the Community and its Member States in international agreements*

As already stated, the joint participation of the Community and its Member States in international agreements ('mixed' agreements) is a Community law requirement.

Does international law also require this practice to be followed in some cases at least?

Jurists in some States consider that the answer to this question is 'Yes' and their influence is not unconnected with the fact that some multilateral agreements have embodied a clause subordinating EEC participation to the complementary participation of all its Member States (for example, the previously-mentioned 1973 Kyoto Convention on the simplification and harmonization of customs procedures) or of a majority of them (for example, the 1982 Convention on the Law of the Sea).

The EEC and its Member States had themselves held the view that the 'mixed' agreement procedure should be used for the conclusion of these agreements. The only question to arise during the negotiation of the said agreements was, therefore, whether this freely-made choice could legally be transformed into an international obligation.

Before considering this point, it may perhaps be useful to assess the practical consequences of the solution adopted for the agreements just mentioned.

It is always difficult for a State to say, at a time when negotiations for an international agreement have not been completed, whether or not it will ratify the agreement in question. It is even more difficult to obtain such an indication from 10 States which have not only to decide whether they will participate in the agreement, in their own right or whether the Community should also be included. The intention or wish of these States to be individual parties to the agreement and the intention and wish that the Community should participate may be based on different considerations and it would appear difficult to demand that they commit themselves, in advance, to linking the two operations.

Insistence that they should do so might have the result that neither the Community nor its Member States would become party to the agreement, which would be contrary to one of the aims generally pursued in the negotiation of multilateral agreements, which is to have them ratified by as many States as possible.

It is clear that, like other international organizations, the Communities have only limited powers and are therefore not entitled to conclude any and every international agreement.

This being so, the Communities have sole responsibility for interpreting the Treaties which set the limits of their powers and the 'draft articles' of the International Law Commission on treaties between States and international organizations or between two or more international organizations confirm that the external powers of such organizations are determined by their 'relevant rules' and 'their established practice'.

However, the draft produced by the International Law Commission (Article 26) (like Article 26 of the Vienna Convention on the Law of Treaties) provides that any treaty in force with respect to an international organization must be enforced by that organization in a spirit of good faith. Such an obligation could not be undertaken by an organization accepting an agreement when it knew from the outset that it would be neither materially nor legally in a position to implement it.

Furthermore, the draft produced by the International Law Commission (Article 46.3) provides (like Article 46 of the Vienna Convention) that 'the fact that the consent of an international organization to be bound by a treaty was given in breach of a provision of the organization's rules regarding powers to conclude treaties cannot be invoked by the organization as invalidating its consent, unless such breach was obvious and involves a rule of fundamental importance'.

Without departing from the proposals of the International Law Commission it would appear that it can be argued that, even without the support of its Member States, the Community could validly participate in agreements partly dealing with matters clearly outside its competence. It would be enough for the Community to attach to its declaration of consent to be bound by such an agreement a statement specifying that its consent covers only matters in the agreement for which it is competent. Such a declaration might not even be necessary.

It can in fact be argued that by accepting the Community as party to a multilateral agreement, the States participating in the negotiation of that agreement have *ipso facto* recognized that the Community could not assume rights and obligations other than in respect of matters covered by the said agreement for which it is clearly not incompetent. And this would apply even if the States were, on their side, required to accept the whole of the agreement or could only restrict their acceptance by reservations such that their participation in the said agreement would, in any case, extend to matters wider than those covered by the Community's commitment. The fact that this commitment might not be supplemented by a commitment from the Member States would not be incompatible with the system of reservations provided for in the agreement.

In the course of the negotiations which raised the question of EEC participation in the future Convention on the Law of the Sea,[1] a view opposite to that just stated was maintained by States which were in favour of establishing a compulsory link between participation by the EEC and by its Member States. The States in question argued that, in the absence of such a link, the Member States of the EEC might find themselves in a privileged position in relation to the other States, because in view of the very limited nature of the reservations allowed by that convention, they would only be able to accept or reject it *en bloc*. By having the EEC participate in the convention and by refraining from ratifying themselves, the Member States would be able to choose to assume only some of the rights and obligations provided for in the convention, which would be contrary to the nature of the package deal it comprised.

To forestall this risk, the States in question sought and obtained agreement for the principle of compulsory joint participation by the EEC and its Member States to be embodied in the text of the convention (Annex IX, Article 2).

The argument on which this decision was based calls for close study. It in fact raises the whole question of the nature of the European Communities in relation to the categories of international law.

---

[1] On this point, see, in particular: J.F. Buhl, *'The European Economic Community and the Law of the Sea'*, Ocean Development and International Law, Vol. 11, Nos 3-4, 1982, pp. 181-200.

If they are deemed to be international organizations with legal personality and powers wholly distinct from those of their Member States, and to be capable of participating independently in international agreements, it is unquestionably not legitimate not to regard them as being 'full' parties and to subordinate their right to participate in such agreements to simultaneous participation by their Member States.

If it is considered, conversely, that by their inclusion in the category of international organization, the Communities together with their Member States, constitute a single entity made up of inseparable components, alone capable of assuming all the rights and obligations stipulated by an agreement, it may be legitimate to require that all subjects of international law forming that entity should jointly sign and, if necessary, ratify (or accept) the agreement. In that case, it would not be sufficient to subordinate participation by the Communities to that of their Member States; the latters' participation would also have to be subordinated to that of the Communities.

We consider, therefore, that there are good arguments both for contesting and defending the thesis that the obligation laid on the Community and its Member States to participate jointly in international agreements not wholly covered by the Community's powers is a requirement of international law.

In any case, it may be observed that the solution adopted in the case of the 1982 Convention on the Law of the Sea (Annex IX, Article 2) constitutes an unsatisfactory compromise since, firstly, it confines itself to linking EEC participation with that of its Member States but does not subordinate the latters' participation to participation by the EEC and, secondly, it requires only that EEC participation shall be combined with that of a majority of its Member States, and moreover accepts that the EEC may remain party to the convention at least so long as at least one of its Member States also does so (Annex IX, Article 8 (c) (ii)).

In our view such provisions have little meaning, because any lack of competence on the part of the EEC to participate alone in an international agreement such as the Convention on the Law of the Sea can validly be made good but by the additional participation of its Member States. In addition, such provisions do not completely satisfy the point argued by certain delegations during the negotiations on the convention, namely that Member States which did not ratify the convention should not be allowed the possibility of using EEC participation as an indirect method of benefiting from the provisions of the convention falling within the competence of the Community, without being required, like the other States, to assume the obligations stipulated in the other provisions of the agreement.

This being so, we consider that the Convention on the Law of the Sea did not constitute a good precedent for resolving the question whether compulsory joint participation by the Communities and their Member States is a requirement of current international law.

B – Notification by the Community of matters in an international agreement for which it is competent

When it is seen that an international agreement will or should be accepted by both the Community and its Member States, other States often indicate that they wish to be informed exactly how the matters covered by the agreement fall within the respective competence of the Community and its Member States.

This concern, which is in itself completely legitimate, has been expressed in strong terms during the negotiations for several agreements and has led a number of States to demand that the clause on Community participation in those agreements should make it obligatory for the Community to submit, when depositing or notifying its instrument of acceptance, a list of the provisions of those agreements which deal with matters within its sphere of competence.

The Community has so far refused to accept such an obligation arguing, firstly, that it would constitute interference in its internal affairs and, secondly, that it could not be properly implemented.

On the first point, the Community's position finds support in the text proposed by the International Law Commission, under the terms of which the extent of an international organization's powers depends on its 'constitutive instruments' and 'its established practice'.

On the second point, the Community's argument is based on the fact that the extent of its powers is likely to change, so that any list which might be provided at a given time would be liable to be wrong some time later.

Moreover, the establishment of such a list would presuppose that the differences of view between Member States as to the exact extent of the Community's international powers had been resolved and this would appear to be a highly unrealistic assumption; furthermore, it would be liable to destroy the advantage frequently offered to the Community and its Member States by the procedure of the 'mixed' agreement, which precisely avoids their having to decide on this difficult issue.

In response to the legitimate concern expressed by certain States, the Community has several times proposed that, instead of what it regards as the excessive and unrealistic obligation to supply a complete list of its powers in respect of matters covered by an international agreement, it should provide States so wishing with information concerning the extent of the rights and obligations which it is assuming in clearly specified cases. This proposal was directed in particular to the case of a dispute with the States in question.

A counter-proposal of this kind was formulated specifically during the negotiations for the previously-mentioned 1979 Convention on the physical protection of nuclear materials and for the 1982 Convention on the Law of the Sea; it was not accepted, with the consequence that both these conventions require the Community to declare its powers in the matters covered by each of them.

The obligation laid on the EAEC by the 1979 Convention raised no insurmountable difficulties. The Court of Justice of the European Communities had in fact already had occasion to rule which provisions of the Convention on the physical protection of nuclear materials fell within the competence of the European Atomic Energy Community and which within the competence of the Member States of the Community.[1]

In the second case, that of the Convention on the Law of the Sea, the EEC has made a declaration specifying the fields in which it has exclusive competence pursuant to express provisions of the Treaty or as the result of the adoption of 'common rules'. In addition, the EEC has been at pains to point out that 'the exercise of the competence that the Member States have transferred to the Community under the Treaties is, by its very nature, subject to continuous development. As a result, the Community reserves the right to make new declarations at a later date.'

Section 5: Community participation in institutions responsible for the implementation and supervision of the international agreements to which it is party

At its own level and with its own means, the Community generally assumes the same rights and obligations as the States by virtue of agreements to which it is party.

There is one area, however, where it sometimes does not find itself on exactly the same footing as the States, namely as regards its participation in institutions responsible for implementation and supervision of the international agreements.

Under many international agreements to which the Community has become party, bodies have been set up for the implementation and supervision of the provisions of those agreements.

This applies, in particular, to most of the bilateral agreements which the Community has concluded with non-member countries and, specifically, to the trade agreements concluded by the Community alone, and to the association and cooperation agreements concluded by both the Community and its Member States (see pp. 64 and 66 above).

Under various names (joint committees, councils of association, cooperation councils, etc.) these agreements have set up managing bodies of which the Community and, where appropriate, its Member States are obviously full members.

---

[1] Opinion 1/78 (Article 103, EAEC) of 14.11.1978, [1978] ECR 2151.

Community participation in these bilateral bodies has not as yet posed any problem within the sphere of application of international law.

The same is not true of its participation in managing bodies set up by multilateral agreements.

It appeared to us useful to take a look at some of the difficulties which this question has raised and at the solutions adopted.

A – *Principle of participation*

The acceptance of the Community as member of the managing bodies for agreements to which it is party has not, generally, raised any special problem. In some cases, however, this question has not been clearly resolved by the Community participation clause incorporated in the agreement. This is so, for example, in the case of the participation clause included in the 1982 Convention on the Law of the Sea,[1] which does not specify whether, by becoming party to the convention, the EEC would be a member of the International Seabed Authority[2] and could be a member of its various institutions (Assembly, Council, etc.).

The actual text of the convention (Article 156.2) in fact explicitly confers the status of member of the Authority only on States which are parties and it is necessary to be a 'member of the Authority' in order to be a member of the Assembly and, where appropriate, of the Council.[3]

Similarly, the already-mentioned 1979 Convention on long-distance transboundary air pollution did not establish clearly on what basis the EEC, which is a party to this agreement, would be allowed to sit on its managing body. This question was discussed in the Economic Commission for Europe after the convention had been signed and it emerged that some parties to the agreement, and in particular the East European countries, held the view that the EEC should participate in that body with only the same status of observer that it holds with the Economic Commission for Europe. It required difficult negotiations to arrive at a compromise between the position held by those countries and that of the EEC which claimed the right to participate on a completely equal footing with the States.

---

[1] Article 305.1 (f) and Annex IX.
[2] Created by Part XI, Section 4 of the convention.
[3] Article 159.1: 'The Assembly shall consist of all members of the Authority. . .'; Article 161.1: 'The Council shall consist of 36 members of the Authority. . .'.

With the exception of these cases, the question of Community participation in managing bodies set up by international agreements has been mainly directed to the terms and conditions of such participation.

B – Terms and conditions of participation

1. Membership of the various bodies

Very often, the managing bodies set up by multilateral agreements include a deliberative assembly, of which all parties to the agreement are full members, and a restricted collegiate body, whose members are elected by the deliberative assembly. Each agreement determines the respective powers of the two institutions and specifies how decisions shall be taken (unanimity or consensus, qualified majority, simple majority, etc.).

Other than in the 'doubtful' cases discussed above, the EEC has always been given the status of member of the deliberative assemblies of the institutions set up by multilateral agreements to which it is party. As a rule, it is also entitled to be elected to membership of the restricted collegiate bodies. In some cases, however, such entitlement has not been granted to the Community. For example, the EEC could not be a member of the 'executive committees' set up under the 1975 Cocoa Agreement and the 1976 Coffee Agreement. Even assuming that it can sit in the 'Assembly' of the International Seabed Authority (see p. 85 above) it will certainly not be able to be a member of the 36-member Council of that Authority. Similarly, the EEC will be able to be a member of the deliberative assembly (Council of Governors) of the Common Commodity Fund set up by the previously-mentioned 1980 Geneva Agreement but it appears certain that it will not be able to be a member of the Fund's 28-member 'Management Board'.

2. Right to vote

The voting rights attached to the status of member of the deliberative assembly and of the restricted collegiate body are allocated sometimes in accordance with the principle of 'one State, one vote' and sometimes by a weighted system.[1] Such a system applies in particular to decisions taken by the managing bodies for world agreements on commodities. The general rule is that each State has a fixed, limited number of 'basic votes' to which are added a number of votes proportionate to its share in output (and exports) or in consumption (and imports) of the product in question. The number of votes so allocated to a single State is also limited to a set absolute ceiling so that it cannot on its own command have a majority within the managing body.

In international bodies of which it is a member, the EEC generally has its own right to vote.

---

[1] See J. Krantz, 'Le vote ponderé dans les organisations internationales', Revue générale de droit international public, Paris, 1981, pp. 314-346.

In bodies set up by agreements to which its Member States are not parties (agreements concluded by the procedure known as 'Community' agreements) the EEC has a right to vote on the same terms and conditions as the States which are parties. If this right is subject to the principle of 'one State, one vote', the EEC has a single vote only. This applies, for example, to its position within the deliberative assembly ('General Council')of the North Atlantic Fisheries Organization set up by the previously-mentioned 1978 convention.

If a weighted voting system is used in the body which manages the agreement, the EEC has a number of base votes and a number of proportional votes, calculated as if it were a State. This is the case, for example, in the 'Council' for the 1979 International olive oil agreement.[1]

When the EEC and its Member States are jointly parties to a multilateral agreement ('mixed' agreement), the question of the Community's right to vote in the managing bodies for that agreement is much more complex. There are two specific problems: the first is which, out of the EEC and its Member States, will be entitled to vote; the second is to determine the 'weight' of the vote which will be cast in one case or the other (assuming, of course, that decisions do not have to be unanimous or arrived at by consensus).

Agreements concluded by the EEC and its Member States have in all cases recognized that the first of these problems (who should vote?) should be resolved in accordance with the power-sharing rules laid down in Community law and consequently that non-member countries should, in all cases, rely on the information they are given by the Community and its Member States.

This being so, the Community's partners have in almost all cases seen fit to stipulate in agreements that if the Community votes on a question, the Member States should refrain from doing so, and conversely.[2] This 'no plural voting' clause is no problem for the Community. Its 'internal law' excludes in principle any 'parallel' or 'concurrent' powers of the EEC and its Member States on the same question.[3]

The second problem (what 'weight' should the Community vote have?) has also been the subject of specific provisions in all agreements.

Once the Community has the status of party to an agreement, it would have been possible to give it one vote only, as in the case when its Member States are not parties. Conversely, it was hardly conceivable that each Member State should not have the right to

---

[1] It should be noted that the proportional votes allocated to the EEC as a 'mainly importing member' are calculated without reference to the volume of olive oil trade between its Member States ('intra-Community trade').

[2] See among other examples, Articles 14.2 of the previously-mentioned 1979 Convention on long-distance transboundary air pollution.

[3] See in particular, Opinion 1/75 (already mentioned) of the Court of Justice of the European Communities ([1975] ECR 1355) handed down with reference to Article 113 of the EEC Treaty (commercial policy).

vote enjoyed by all the States. It would then have been necessary to stipulate that, in cases where the Community was entitled to vote, it should have one vote and that, in cases where the Member States were entitled to vote, their number of votes would equal the number of them who were parties to the agreement. This arrangement was rejected because it would have created an imbalance between votes cast by the Community and by its Member States, which would not reflect any political and economic reality. The adoption of this system would moreover have provided an incentive for the Community and its Member States to use the latters' vote systematically at the expense of the former's and would have tempted non-member countries to apply the opposite solution. The rules of Community law and their autonomous status could only have suffered as a result.

To avoid these problems the negotiators of agreements adopted a 'neutral' system under which the EEC receives a number of votes equal to the total number of votes available to its Member States which are parties to the agreement. This rule has been applied both for the bodies working under the principle of 'one State, one vote'[1] and for those where a weighted voting system is used.[2]

The 1980 Canberra Convention (mentioned previously) on the conservation of Antarctic marine fauna and flora makes a limited exception to this rule. In this case, the EEC will have only one vote in the 'Commission' set up by the convention,[3] where it will sit together with some of its Member States. In the event of a vote, there is consequently the possibility of an imbalance between votes on questions for which the Community is competent and votes on other questions. In practice, this is hardly like to occur because most decisions will have to be arrived at by consensus.[4] Furthermore, the negotiators had chiefly in mind the case, peculiar to this convention, where the 'Commission' would have to adopt, particularly with regard to the conservation of fishery resources, measures applying both to areas of ocean within the territorial jurisdiction of the EEC and to areas of ocean not within the territorial field of application of the EEC Treaty, as for example, the waters near Kerguelen and Crozet, which are within the jurisdiction of France. For such a case, the convention provides that the EEC's vote shall be added to that of its Member States which are members of the Commission; the total number of such votes may not however exceed the number of Member States of the EEC which are members of the Commission.[5] The result is that, if the EEC votes, one Member State will have to abstain! It will be seen that with this fairly complex system, the application of which may give rise to delicate problems, the Canberra Convention envisages a possibility of 'plural' voting not envisaged by the other multilateral agreements to which the EEC and its Member States are parties. To that extent, it does not constitute a precedent opposed to the 'neutrality' rule adopted in those agreements.

---

[1] See for example, 1974 Paris Convention (mentioned previously) on the prevention of marine pollution from land-based sources, Article 19.

[2] See for example the 1979 International natural rubber agreement (mentioned previously), Article 5.2.

[3] Article XII.4 of the convention.

[4] Article XII.1 of the convention.

[5] Article XII.3 of the convention.

Chapter II – Participation by the European Communities in acts and decisions of international law other than treaties

This chapter considers decisions, resolutions, declarations, recommendations, etc. embodying the conclusions of various negotiations conducted in international organizations and at international conferences, at both world and regional level.

These instruments whose content, conditions of adoption, forms and effects are as varied as the institutions and circumstances which produce them have very little by way of common denominator, except that in general they impose on the accepting parties obligations of a much more flexible character than those resulting from treaties and leave the parties much wider discretion regarding methods of implementation.

The exact scope of the commitments they involve is by no means always clear, particularly when they emanate from texts deliberately described (final act, charter, code of conduct, etc.) and drafted in ambiguous terms in order to help reach a compromise between the opposing views of the interested parties.

'Models' of such compromises are the various resolutions of the General Assembly of the United Nations on the establishment of a 'new international economic order', the Final Act of the Conference on Security and Cooperation in Europe (Helsinki, 1975),[1] the Code for the control of restrictive business practices (United Nations, 1980).[2]

The activity of international organizations and conferences is clearly not confined to exercises of diplomatic virtuosity and also includes, in many areas, the adoption of instruments whose scope is clearly defined.

Wherever the decisions, resolutions, declarations or recommendations of international organizations and conferences relate to matters within their competence and wherever

---

[1] See, in particular, J.F. Prévost, *'Observations sur la nature juridique de l'acte final de la CSCE',* Annuaire français de droit international, 1975, pp. 129-153.

[2] Doc. Unctad TD/RBP/CONF/10 of 2.5.1980. On this 'code' and other codes now being drafted (transfer of technology, transnational companies, etc) see W. Fikentscher, *'United Nations Codes of Conduct: New paths in international law',* the American Journal of Comparative law, Vol. 30, No 4, 1982, pp. 577-604.

their status with such institutions ensures them the necessary means, the European Communities participate in the drafting and adoption of such instruments (Section 1) and in their implementation (Section 2).

Section 1: Participation of the European Communities in the drafting and adoption of acts and decisions of international organizations and conferences

Everything said in the first part of this study concerning participation by the Communities in negotiations conducted in international organizations and conferences applies, in particular, to such negotiations which culminate in the adoption of decisions, resolutions, declarations or recommendations. Nothing further need be said here, therefore, concerning the terms on which the Communities take part in the drafting of such instruments.

By contrast, participation by the Communities in the adoption of these instruments raises specific problems which have not yet been discussed.

When one or other of the Communities is a member of an international organization or body and has the right to vote, it is usually entitled *ipso facto* to take part, within the limits of its powers, in the adoption of instruments submitted to those organizations or bodies for approval. All the points made in Chapter 1 of the present Part Two (p. 86 *et seq.)* concerning the Communities' right to vote in bodies set up by agreements to which they are party also apply to the case now considered.

There is nothing to add. It simply has to be recalled that the international organizations or bodies in which the Communities have the right to vote are few in number (managing bodies for world agreements on basic commodities and commissions for regional fisheries organizations in particular).

In most international organizations (UN institutions and special agencies, OECD, Council of Europe, etc.) the Communities attend only as observers without voting rights.

Normally, therefore, they can take no part in the adoption of instruments emanating from those organizations.

It has to be considered whether this state of affairs is compatible with the requirements of Community law and, if not, to consider how this incompatibility can be resolved, as and when necessary.

A – Requirements of Community law

In its Opinion 1/78 (previously mentioned) handed down on 4 November 1979 concerning the compatibility of the International Natural Rubber Agreement, worked out withing Unctad, with the provisions of the EEC Treaty, the Court of Justice of the European Communities maintained that Article 116 of the EEC Treaty 'was framed so that the Member States should take common action in international organizations to which the Community does not belong'.

'In these circumstances', declared the Court, 'the only appropriate means is concerted joint action by the Member States, as members of the said organizations'. The Court added, however, that when 'negotiations started in an international organization are intended to culminate in a binding commitment entered into by subjects of international law, the provisions of the Treaty relating to the negotiation and conclusion of agreements apply, or in other words Articles 113, 114 and 228 and not Article 116'.

This opinion of the Court of Justice raises at least two questions.

If the purpose of negotiations started in an international organization is to arrive at 'a binding commitment', does the Court's opinion mean that the Community should take part not only in the drafting of the commitment (negotiations) and its implementation (conclusion) but also in the adoption of the resolution or final act whereby the organization approves and authenticates the terms which have been negotiated? What if, in view of its status as observer without voting rights, the Community is not allowed to be party to that decision? Must it then be considered that the Member States can validly take its place?

Practice has moved in that direction and it does not appear that Opinion 1/78 should be regarded taking the opposite view. This point will be further considered later.

The second question raised by this opinion is whether it should be interpreted by contrary argument as meaning that 'concerted joint action by the Member States' is sufficient to cover the instruments of international organizations which, although concerned with matters within the Community's sphere of competence, do not involve a 'binding commitment' for the subjects of international law to which they are addressed.

It may be doubted whether the Court's opinion gives an affirmative reply to this question.

The first point to be made is that the Court confined itself to saying that Article 116 'was framed so that the Member States should take common action in international organizations to which the Community does not belong' and to deciding that the negotiation and conclusion of an agreement involving a binding commitment were not covered by the provisions of that article. It would no doubt be going too far to argue *a contrario* to draw any consequence whatsoever from that decision, as the case of instruments of international law other than treaties or agreements has never been referred to the Court.

Any other view would be tantamount to recognizing that notwithstanding the rule 'who can do the most can do the least', the Community has the powers to negotiate and conclude binding agreements but not agreements which are not binding. In our view, such an interpretation would proceed from a mistakenly literal interpretation of Articles 113, 114 and 228, which apply to genuine 'agreements' only. It would moreover involve establishing in each case whether the intended commitment is binding or not.

As the scope of the instruments in question is sometimes deliberately 'camouflaged' such a procedure would be legally pointless and politically inopportune.

Furthermore, interpretation *a contrario* which we reject would have the unsatisfactory result that the extent of the Community's powers would depend on whether or not it is in actual fact a member of an international organization at a given point in time.

Lastly, it has to be remembered that some resolutions adopted by international organizations and in particular by the General Assembly of the United Nations, are directed not only to States but also to 'groups of States' which have powers in the areas covered by their provisions (1974 Charter of States' economic rights and duties, Article 12; 1980 'Code' for the monitoring of restrictive business practices, section B.8) These clauses unequivocally refer to the European Communities.

For all these reasons, we consider that Community law theoretically requires that the Communities themselves should take part in the drafting, adoption and implementation of decisions, resolutions, etc. adopted by international organizations and conferences which relate to matters within their competence.

Practice is to a large extent in accordance with this requirement.

B – *Solutions in practice*

As shown in Part One, Community representatives have relatively satisfactory rights to speak in organizations and at conferences of which the Community is not a member and they use this right in all negotiations, particularly in those for the adoption by these organizations and conferences of decisions, resolutions, declarations and recommendations.

It will be shown later (Section 2 below) that some of these instruments are implemented by the Community without any objections being raised to this practice.

Apart from certain special cases which will be discussed later, the Community is not, on the other hand, allowed to take part itself in the adoption of instruments by organizations and conferences of which it is not a member, so that its Member States have to participate in its place. The Court of Justice has given no explicit ruling as to whether such substitution is in conformity with Community law, but its Opinion 1/78 would seem to indicate that 'concerted, joint action' by the Member States can validly take the place of genuine Community action when the latter is prevented. The affirmation that the application of Article 116 is the 'only appropriate means' of resolving problems arising from the fact that the Community is not a member of certain international organizations, would seem to tend towards such an internpretation. It should be noted further that in a ruling prior to Opinion 1/78,[1] the Court seems to have accepted that, where the Community is not a member of an international organization dealing with matters for which it has exclusive competence, its Member States can continue to take part in the work and decisions of that organization, provided they comply with the requirements of Article 116 of the EEC Treaty and provided 'they use all legal and political means at their disposal' to bring about the subsequent admission of the Community to membership of the organization.

In any event, the problem we have raised is of fairly limited significance, because most instruments emanating from international organizations and conferences are adopted by consensus without a vote. Since, despite its limited observer status, the Community is able to take part in the drafting of such instruments and since account is taken of the views stated by its representatives during the negotiations, the question of its participation in the adoption of such instruments is, in this case, of theoretical interest only.

In a number of cases, the Community has been allowed to participate more or less directly in the adoption of instruments of international organizations of which it is not a member.

The first case is that of GATT. The EEC does not have the formal status of 'contracting party' to the General Agreement and in theory does not have the right to vote in GATT bodies. It has been recognized, however, that it has taken the place of its Member States for all matters relating to commercial policy questions dealt with by the organization.[2] Consequently, instruments adopted by GATT institutions on such matters can be regarded as having been adopted by the EEC, among others. The question has, however, never been cleared up because decisions by the 'contracting parties' are always taken by consensus.

Mention should also be made of the circumstances in which the EEC was able to take part in the adoption of the Final Act of the Conference on Security and Cooperation in Europe (Helsinki, 1975).

It is generally known that the EEC was not invited to participate in this conference in any capacity and that its representatives were only able to attend and speak by joining the delegation of the State holding the presidency of the Council of the Communities. At the final session of the Conference, the representative of the State concerned – which was Italy at the time – declared that 'the conclusions of the Conference will be implemented (in relation to non-member countries) by the Communities in respect of matters for which they are at present, or will subsequently be, competent' and that 'in respect of

---

[1] Judgment of 14.7.1976, Joined Cases 3, 4 and 6/76 *Kramer* (1976) ECR 1279 *et seq.*

[2] See the previously-mentioned judgment of the Court of Justice of 12.12.1972 in the *International Fruit* case, Joined Cases 21 to 24/72.

such matters the expression 'participating States' appearing in the Final Act will be understood as applying also to the European Communities'. He consequently informed the other participants that he would sign the Final Act of the conference 'in (his) dual capacity as the representative of Italy for that country and as President-in-Office of the Council of the European Communities for those Communities'.[1] The Helsinki Final Act in fact carries the signature of Aldo Moro as Prime Minister of the Italian Republic and as President of the Council of the European Communities.

No objections were raised to either Mr Moro's declaration or his signature, even by the USSR and the other East European countries, which no doubt concluded that opposition to this clear demonstration of the unity of the EEC and its Member States might delay or jeopardize the conclusion of the conference.

Section 2: Participation by the European Communities in the implementation of acts and decisions of international organizations and conferences

A – Acts and decisions of organizations and conferences of which the Communities are members

When an international organization adopts a decision, resolution or recommendation, the members of the organization are naturally required either to take the necessary measures to execute that instrument, if it imposes such an obligation on them, or to decide what action to take upon it if it does not contain any binding provisions.

This rule applies equally to the States and to the European Communities when the latter are members of the organization and the decision, resolution or recommendation is concerned with matters for which they are competent.

There are many practical examples of measures taken by one or other of the Communities and, in particular, by the EEC to implement acts and decisions adopted by international organizations or bodies of which it is a member.

The commonest case is that of regulations or decisions of the Council of the Communities designed to implement, within the Community, the decisions or recommendations of mixed committees, association councils and cooperation councils set up under bilateral agreements to which the EEC is party.

---

[1] See *Ninth General Report on the Activities of the European Communities – 1975* (Office for Official Publications of the European Communities, Luxembourg) point 511, p. 300.

There are also examples of EEC regulations or decisions approving or accepting acts and decisions adopted by the managing bodies for multilateral agreements to which the EEC is party. We shall quote, for example, the Council Decision of 24 June 1982, accepting, on behalf of the EEC, a recommendation by the International Commission for the protection of the Rhine against pollution.[1]

B – Acts and decisions of organizations and conferences of which the Communities are not members

Intervention by the European Communities in the implementation of acts and decisions adopted by international organizations or conferences of which they are not members but concerned with matters within their competence raises delicate problems.

When such acts and decisions are binding on the members of the organization and in particular on the Member States of the Communities can they also be considered to be binding on the Communities?

Whether or not such acts and decisions are binding on the members of the organization, can the Communities legitimately take the place of their Member States in adopting the measures necessary for their execution or in deciding what action should be taken on them?

The first of these questions arose in the case of the embargo on exports to South Africa and the former Southern Rhodesia, ordered by the Security Council under Article 41 of the United Nations Charter.[2] In the case of measures which may come within the competence of the EEC under the terms of Article 113 of the establishing Treaty, it could be asked whether, under the terms of that article and taken in conjunction with the provisions of Article 48 of the charter which requires the Member States of the United Nations to take the necessary measures to implement decisions of the Security Council,[3] this was not also an obligation for the EEC. This question was not resolved, because the Member States of the EEC considered that they were required to apply the 'trade sanctions' ordered by the United Nations Security Council against South Africa

---

[1] OJ L 210, 1982.

[2] 'The Security Council may decide what measures. . . should be taken to implement its decisions and may invite the Members of the United Nations to apply those measures. Such measures may include the complete or partial breaking off of economic relations. . .'.

[3] '1. The measures required to implement the decisions of the Security Council for the maintenance of international peace and security shall be taken by all members of the United Nations or by some of them, at the discretion of the Council.

2. Such decisions shall be implemented by the Members of the United Nations directly and, by their action in the appropriate international bodies to which they belong'.

and the former Southern Rhodesia, not by way of EEC regulations or decisions but by national measures under the terms of Article 224 of the EEC Treaty.[1,2]

Can the Community validly take the place of its Member States for the implementation of instruments adopted by international organizations of which it is not a member, whether or not those instruments are binding on those States?

This question can easily be answered in the affirmative when the implementation (or non-implementation) of the instrument does not involve, for the Member States of the organization, any obligatory procedure such as notification of formal acceptance (or of an objection), transmission of a report on measures to implement the instrument or stating reasons for not implementing, etc.

In the event of a dispute concerning the implementation of a binding instrument, the Member States of the Community, bound by that instrument, would simply have to prove that they had properly fulfilled their obligations, including by way of measures taken in their place by the Community. In view of the known legal effects of Community instruments in respect of their Member States, such proof could easily be provided, subject of course to the proviso that the substance of the measures taken by the Community is in conformity with the instrument to be implemented.

When the member States of an international organization are required, by an instrument of that organization, to fulfil procedural obligations of the kind described in the previous paragraph, a further question arises, namely, whether the Community is 'admissible' for the purpose of discharging those obligations for and on behalf of its Member States.

In several cases, the Council of the Communities has taken the view that it was in the interests of the EEC to implement recommendations or resolutions adopted by international organizations of which the Community is not a member, but concerned, wholly or in part, with matters within its competence. These recommendations and resolutions laid down a formal procedure for acceptance by members of the organization. In consequence, the Council of the Communities instructed its president to notify the secretariat of the organization that the recommendation or resolution was accepted by the EEC and also at the same time by all the Member States.

Such notifications were sent to the Secretariat of the United Nations Economic Commission for Europe (acceptance of Resolution 119, revised, on the standardization of forms used for licences for the international transport of goods by road) and to the secre-

---

[1] Article 224: 'Member States shall consult each other with a view to taking together the steps needed to prevent the functioning of the common market being affected by measures which a Member State may be called upon to take. . . in order to carry out obligations it has accepted for the purpose of maintaining peace and international security.' Similarly, when the American hostages were seized at the United States embassy in Tehran, the Member States acted against Iran in the framework of political cooperation and under the terms of Article 224 (cf. Bulletin EC 5-1980, p. 27 et seq.).

[2] Cf. P.J. Kuyper, 'Sanctions against Rhodesia, the EEC and the implementation of general international legal rules', Common Market Law Review, 1975, pp. 231-244.

tariat of the 'Codex alimentarius' ('Standards for the production and marketing of various food products'). These notifications were 'received' by the addressees without objection.

So far as we know, there have been no cases where the 'admissibility' of a procedural act carried out by the Community has been challenged.

PART THREE

The European Communities and the application of international law

The Communities are subject to international law. In this part, consideration is given to the special difficulties created by the specific nature of the Communities as regards the application to them of the rules of international law.

These difficulties may arise in connection with:

  (i)   the implementation of international agreements (Chapter 1);

 (ii)   international responsibility (Chapter 2);

(iii)   the peaceful settlement of disputes (Chapter 3).

Chapter I – The Communities and the implementation of international agreements

The agreement is the principal instrument of international transactions.

Although agreements are in most cases arrived at by a codified, formal procedure, they may also be concluded by informal procedures.

The Court of Justice of the European Communities took account of the reality of international practice when it defined the agreement in broad terms as 'any binding commitment entered into by subjects of international law, whatever the formal title attaching to it'.[1]

International agreements are governed by a set of customary rules, most of which are codified in the Vienna Convention of 23 May 1969 on the Law of Treaties.[2]

Admittedly, this convention is supposed to apply only to a particular category of agreements, namely to treaties between States. In fact, however, it defines in essence a system of references which, with certain adaptations can be applied to all international agreements.

This interpretation was confirmed, if confirmation were needed, by the fact that the International Law Commission, when studying the question of treaties concluded between States and international organizations or between two or more international organizations, decided to rely on the Vienna Convention on the Law of Treaties and, in the draft articles formulated on this subject, to transpose it, as far as possible, to agreements to which international organizations are parties.[3]

---

[1] Opinion 1/75, 11.11.1975, ECR 1355.

[2] The Vienna Convention as such applies only to States party to it. However, in the case of provisions agreed by a consensus (the most numerous) it may be considered that, as the express international custom, they are of general application.

[3] Like the Vienna Convention, the ILC project does not cover a number of questions such as the relationships between agreements and subsequent agreements or the relationship between the implementation of agreements and international responsibility. For details of the drafting of the project and of its present state see the ILC report to the General Assembly on its 34th Session (1982) A/37/10. The terms of the draft quoted in the study are extracted from that document. cf. P. Reuter, 'Le droit des traités et les accords internationaux conclus par les organisations internationales', in Miscellanea W.J. Ganshof van der Meersch, 1972, Vol. 1, pp. 195-275.

This 'common fund' of law on international agreements applies to Community agreements.

It is revealing in this respect that when the Communities had to comment on the ILC draft they considered it to be generally satisfactory, with one or two reservations.[1]

For that reason, although the ILC text on this point still lacks any intrinsic legal authority, our discussion of the problems will take account wherever possible of the terms of the text.

As in the previous sections, the general rule is set against the specific nature of the Communities and the difficulties which can result are explained.

Without claiming to offer an exhaustive list, it would appear that the difficulties may relate to the following points, each of which will be dealt with in one of the following sections:

(i)   Successive agreements which are incompatible;

(ii) Scope of agreements in internal Community law and in the law of Member States;

(iii) Respect for Community powers and nullity of agreements;

(iv) Implementation of Community agreements by Member States;

(v)   Grounds claimed by the Community for the suspension or interruption of agreements;

(vi) Territorial area of application of agreements.

Section 1: Successive agreements which are incompatible

One of the classical problems of treaty law is the total or partial incompatibility of agreements successively concluded by the same State with different parties.

The Vienna Convention adopted useful reference rules on this point. These have been transferred by the ILC into its draft in the following terms (Article 30):

'When a treaty specifies that it is subordinate to a preceding or subsequent treaty or that it should not be deemed incompatible with that other treaty, the provisions of that treaty shall prevail.

When all the parties to the preceding treaty are also parties to the subsequent treaty, even though the preceding treaty is still in force or its application has not been suspended under the terms of Article 59, the preceding treaty shall apply only insofar as its provisions are compatible with those of the subsequent treaty.

---

[1] See the comments of the EEC reproduced in Annex II to the ILC report on its 33rd Session (1981) A/36/10, p. 892.

When the parties to the preceding treaty are not all parties to the subsequent treaty:

(a) for the purpose of relations between two parties which are both parties to both treaties, the rule laid down in paragraph 3 shall apply;

(b) for the purpose of relations between a party to both treaties and a party to one of those treaties only, the treaty to which they are both parties determines their mutual rights and obligations;

(c) paragraph 4 shall apply without prejudice to Article 41, to any question or to any suspension of the application of the treaty under the terms of Article 60, or any question of responsibility which may arise for a State or an international organization through the conclusion or implementation of a treaty the provisions of which are incompatible with its obligations towards another State or organization, or, as appropriate, towards another organization or State not party to the said treaty, under the terms of another treaty.'

Such provisions apply one of the basic principles of the law of contract, namely that of 'relative effect' *(res inter alios acta)* according to which an agreement cannot be invoked against a third party. Logically, therefore, it leads to the maintenance of all agreements. When such maintenance is impossible because the implementation of one is a continuing violation of the other, the party to both agreements has no option but to abandon one or the other. But as it cannot claim its participation in one of the agreements as lawful grounds for denouncing the other, it can be sued by the partners who would be prejudiced by its withdrawal.

Faced with such a problem, the Communities may find themselves in exactly the same situation as a State. This is the case if a Community has become party to successive agreements which are incompatible. The Communities are not therefore in a special situation which could give rise to fresh difficulties.

On the other hand, its special nature comes up again when the question arises of the relationship between Community Treaties and treaties concluded by one (or more) Member States.

The analysis becomes more complicated according to whether the case is that of incompatibility between an agreement concluded previously by a Member State and the Treaties establishing the Communities (A) or that of incompatibility between an agreement concluded previously by a Member State and an agreement concluded by the Community (B). The case of incompatibility between an agreement concluded by the Community and an agreement subsequently entered into by a Member State will also have to be considered (C).

A – Incompatibility between the Treaties establishing the Communities and an agreement previously entered into by a Member State

The difficulties are less if the preceding agreement was concluded between Member States than if it concerns one or more Member States and one or more non-member States.

1. Agreement between Member States

(a) The obligation not to conclude or to end an incompatible agreement concluded between Member States

Under the terms of paragraph 2 of Article 5 of the EEC Treaty 'Member States shall abstain from any measure which could jeopardize the attainment of the objectives of this Treaty'.[1]

On this basis alone, the conclusion between Member States of an agreement incompatible with Community law might be regarded as a 'breach' of that law.

It would also be so if it constituted an encroachment by Member States on Community powers in the field of international relationships.

As these rules apply both in respect of the establishing Treaties and of law derived from them, they go much further than a standard clause specifying that the establishing Treaties take precedence over any agreement concluded between Member States.

(b) Special case: Article 233 of the EEC Treaty and Article 202 of the EAEC Treaty

Articles 233 of the EEC Treaty and 202 of the EAEC Treaty stipulate: 'The provisions of this Treaty shall not preclude the existence or completion of regional unions between Belgium and Luxembourg, or between Belgium, Luxembourg and the Netherlands, to the extent that the objectives of these regional unions are not attained by application of this Treaty'.

These articles do not really constitute an exception to the general rule stated above, to the extent that the regional agreements in question are not considered to be incompatible with the EEC and EAEC Treaties. At the same time they guarantee to the members of these unions that they can continue to pursue their objectives and go further in the context of their regional union than in that of the Community itself.

2. Agreements between Member States and non-member States

The Treaties establishing the Communities cannot themselves impose any obligations on non-member countries. On the other hand, they can require Member States to seek to reduce the difficulties arising from the incompatibility of some of their provisions with those of agreements concluded previously by Member States with non-member States.

---

[1] Article 192 of the EAEC Treaty is worded identically. The wording of the ECSC Treaty is slightly narrower. Paragraph 2 of Article 86 reads: 'Member States undertake to refrain from any measures incompatible with the existence of the common market referred to in Articles 1 and 4.'

The problem is dealt with differently in the EEC Treaty (Article 234) and the EAEC Treaty (Article 105).

(a) Article 234 of the EEC Treaty

'The rights and obligations arising from agreements concluded before the entry into force of this Treaty between one or more Member States on the one hand, and one or more third countries on the other, shall not be affected by the provisions of this Treaty.

To the extent that such agreements are not compatible with this Treaty, the Member State or States concerned shall take all appropriate steps to eliminate the incompatibilities established. Member States shall, where necessary, assist each other to this end and shall, where appropriate, adopt a common attitude.

In applying the agreements referred to in the first paragraph, Member States shall take into account the fact that the advantages accorded under this Treaty by each Member State form an integral part of the establishment of the Community and are thereby inseparably linked with the creation of common institutions, the conferring of powers upon them and the granting of the same advantages by all the other Member States.'

Paragraph 1 of Article 234 simply enunciates a rule deriving from customary law. The rights of third countries (and by corollary the obligations of Member States) are not reduced nor *a fortiori* abrogated by the conclusion of the EEC Treaty. For non-member countries this is in fact a 'relative effect' *(res inter alios acta).*

This paragraph would go beyond customary law if it meant that the Member States of the EEC can rely in their dealings with each other (and contrary to Community law) on the provisions of agreements previously concluded with non-member countries. But the Court of Justice of the European Communities rejected this interpretation and ruled that the sole purpose of Article 234 was 'to safeguard the rights of non-member States'.[1]

The second paragraph specifies action required of the Member States. It can affect non-member countries only through the action of the Member States.

It in fact envisages the kind of situation mentioned earlier, where it is impossible to maintain participation in two incompatible relationships under agreement, and, as is normal, calls on Member States to resolve the conflict in favour of the EEC Treaty.

The third paragraph has nothing in common with the traditional rules of international law because it is based on the specific nature of Community relationships. It appears *a priori* as a recommendation to Member States to place a restrictive interpretation on agreements they have concluded with non-member countries. In fact, these provisions can be understood only if set against the most-favoured nation clauses included in

---

[1] Case 10/61 *Commission* V *Italy,* ECR Vol. VIII, p. 22.

many agreements. The strict application of such clauses would have had the practical effect of extending whole areas of intra-Community relationships to non-member countries, particularly in the matter of trade relations, by extending to beneficiaries of the most-favoured nation clause the rules for the removal of customs barriers between Member States.

In practice, the Member States have prevented this from happening not by relying directly on this paragraph – which again cannot be used against third countries – but by invoking a provision of the GATT – the customs union exception (Article XXIV) – which allows the members of a customs union (or of a free-trade area) not to apply to third countries the special system established between them. In view of this Community attitude, non-member countries had to put a brave face on the matter, but did not hold back from criticizing the excessive 'protectionism' of the Community, taking the place of the protectionism of individual Member States.[1]

At this point the quarrel ceased to be a legal issue and called only for a political reply which was given by the Community during the major tariff negotiations conducted under the auspices of GATT (Kennedy Round and its continuation).

(b) Article 105 of the EAEC Treaty

Article 105 of the EAEC Treaty reads: 'The provisions of this Treaty shall not be invoked so as to prevent the implementation of agreements or contracts concluded before its entry into force by a Member State, a person or an undertaking with a third State . . . where such agreements or contracts have been communicated to the Commission not later than thirty days after the entry into force of this Treaty.

Agreements or contracts concluded between the signature and the entry into force of this Treaty by a person or an undertaking with a third State, an international organization or a national of a third State shall not, however, be invoked as grounds for failure to implement this Treaty if, in the opinion of the Court of Justice, ruling on an application from the Commission, one of the decisive reasons on the part of either of the parties in concluding the agreement or contract was an intention to evade the provisions of this Treaty.'

---

[1] The quarrel was also carried into the International Law Commission when it sought to 'codify' the rules for the system of the most-favoured nation clause.

Led by the Soviet member of the commission, a number of members argued that the 'customs union exception' clause, as it appears in the GATT, could not be a general rule capable of being included in a codifying text.

The first ILC draft contains no provision on this point.

In its comments, the Community strongly criticized this deficiency and called for the addition of an article specifying that rights and obligations established within economic unions, customs unions or free-trade areas are not affected. See the annex to the ILC's report to the General Assembly on its 30th session (1977) Doc. A/33/10, pp. 179-184.

The text of the articles adopted by the Commission also appears in that document (p. 16 *et seq.*). In its introduction, the Commission states that it has left pending the question of customs unions, so that the decision on this point may be taken by the States which will have to decide on the draft (ibid. pp. 13 and 14).

Under the terms of paragraph 1, a Member State can invoke a provision of an agreement which it has concluded before the entry into force of the EAEC Treaty only if it has declared the existence of that agreement to the Commission within a certain time after the entry into force of the EAEC Treaty.

This provision protects the rights of third parties.

It also has to be deduced, however, that if a Member State has deliberately or otherwise failed to comply with this formality, it is required to apply the EAEC Treaty without being able to plead its previous commitments.

It is required to cease applying the provisions of previous agreements, to the extent that they are incompatible with the EAEC Treaty.

It may then be sued by the States parties to the agreements which it has to denounce.

B – Incompatibility between a previous agreement concluded between Member States and non-member States and an agreement concluded by the Communities

By limiting itself to the problem of incompatibility between previous agreements concluded by Member States and the EEC Treaty itself, Article 234 ignored the true extent of the problem. This emerged as the number of international agreements entered into by the Communities increased.

As the Communities acquire powers to conclude international agreements in areas within their competence, agreements which they conclude may be contrary to previous agreements concluded by Member States on the same subject.

The problem of the incompatibility of subsequent treaties is then complicated by the problem of succession.

In international law, the term 'succession' in the expressions 'succession of States' or 'succession of international organizations' applies to the substitution of one subject of law for another, without the implication that the 'successor' automatically inherits the rights and obligations of the subject it succeeds.

The formula applies to the European Communities in relation to their Member States, with the proviso that such succession is partial or by categories and not total. The position is that the Communities take the place of the States and deal with third parties on all matters for which powers have been transferred to them by the States, by virtue of Community principles.

The central question regarding the effect of succession on treaties is whether the substitution of one subject of law for another constitutes legitimate grounds for breaking a treaty link.

The customary rules of international law have never been absolutely clear on this point. It is accepted, however, that since 'decolonization', the principle of the continuity of undertakings given has been yielding to that of the fresh start or at least the free choice of a successor.[1] Each case of succession is specific, however. In the case of the Communities, the problem should not be stated in such clear-cut terms. The political and even the philosophical background which makes the problem so complicated in the case of States, is absent. Furthermore, the Communities obviously cannot invoke the 'sovereignty' which automatically accrues to every new State.

Despite the different context, the question is still a major embarrassment because a balance has to be found between respect for the rights of third parties and the autonomy of the new institution.

The question remained latent for a long time until it was brought to the fore by a series of disputes in which the Court of Justice of the European Communities became involved.

The Court's rulings enunciated a principle but could not be applied in full to an international dispute between the Community and a non-member State.

1. Case-law of the Court of Justice of the European Communities: rejection of 'succession'

In the first case on 'Fisheries: rights of non-member countries' (1980), the Court ruled on an interlocutory question from the Circuit Court of the County of Cork which had to deal with a case of illegal fishing by a Spanish owner in Irish waters.

The defendant based his defence on the provisions of the London Agreement to which Ireland – a Member State – and Spain – a non-member State – were parties and argued that this agreement should be deemed to be still in force, by virtue of the terms of Article 234 of the EEC Treaty.

Although the question was not put in such clear terms, an affirmative ruling by the Court would have meant that the Community which was not party to the London Agreement, was bound by it by virtue of Article 234.

However, the Court considered that while Article 234 required the Community institutions 'not to impede the execution of the obligations of Member States arising from a previous agreement' the intention was 'only that the Member State concerned should

---

[1] H.G. Schermers, *'Succession of States and international organizations'*, Netherlands Yearbook of International Law, 1975, (pp. 103-11).

be able to fulfil its obligations under the previous agreement, *without the Community being bound thereby as regards the State concerned.*[1]

This would suggest that the Community is not bound by agreements previously concluded by Member States on the sole grounds that such agreements were concluded on matters within Community competence. It may be concluded from this that the machinery for access by succession to an agreement previously concluded by the Member States, as accepted by the Court in its *International Fruit* ruling,[2] is not of general application and in any case cannot be brought under Article 234.

Referring specifically to this ruling, the Advocate General, Mr Capotorti, made it quite clear that the Community had succeeded to the obligations of Member States under the GATT: 'not solely on the basis of the single fact that it had taken over powers previously exercised by the Member States in the matter governed by the General Agreement but also taking account of at least four other decisive elements: the fact that the Member States were already bound by the GATT when they concluded the EEC Treaty, the consent of the same States to bind the Community by the obligations of the Agreement coinciding with the acceptance by the Community of the aims of the GATT by virtue of Article 110 of the Treaty of Rome, the action in fact taken by the Community institutions in the framework of that Agreement and the recognition, by the other contracting parties, of the transfer of powers by Member States to the Community'.[3] The issue was therefore to show clearly that the GATT case was specific.

In the fisheries case, the Court also gave a very broad application to the precedence of Community provisions over the previous agreement concluded by the Member States.

The Court in fact considered that, in the area in question, despite the provisions of the earlier agreement, the provisions of interim *Community regulations* applied, pending a fisheries agreement with the non-member State concerned, namely Spain, adding that these regulations 'came within the framework of relations between the Community and Spain . . .'.[4]

In this case, the Court did not intend to say however that the system set up by Community law had taken the place of the previous system. It ruled that the two systems were 'superimposed'. The logic of this ruling may be open to criticism, because incompatible provisions cannot be superimposed, as one must of necessity prevail over the other in accordance with a criterion to be defined.

---

[1] Judgment of the Court of Justice of 14.10.1980, Case 812/79 *Burgoa* [1980] ECR 2787.

[2] Judgment of 12.12.1972, Joined Cases 21 to 24/72 *International Fruit* [1972] ECR 1219; judgment of 24.10.1973, Case 9/73 *Shluter* [1973] ECR 1135; judgment of 19.11.1975, Case 38/75 *Nederlandse Spoorwegen* [1975] ECR 1439.

[3] Findings, Case 812/79, quoted in note 1 above.

[4] Judgment of 14.10.1980, Case 812/79, previously mentioned. See note by H. Schermers, 18 *Common Market Law Review*, 1981, pp. 227-231; see also by the same author, *'Rights-giving Treaties: Higher Law'*, in Mélanges en l' honneur de P.H. Teitgen, Pedone, Paris, 1984.

By contrast, in other later cases arising from the same sort of circumstances, but involving agreements concluded between Spain and France, where Article 234 could not be invoked, as the agreements in question had been concluded after the EEC Treaty came into force, the Court took the view that the legal rules resulting from the relations established between the Community and Spain had 'replaced' those resulting from the Franco-Spanish agreements.[1]

In any event, it emerges from these decisions that the Court largely took the view that the Communities are free agents within their treaty powers, despite the existence of previous agreements concluded by the Member States.

It may be felt that this line of argument takes little account of the rights of non-member States.

In these cases, however, the Court gave judgment, not as an international court but as a Community court, ruling at the request of a national court.

These decisions do not, therefore, prejudge the manner in which a dispute between the Community and a non-member State should be resolved in a case for which the Court of Justice of the European Communities was not the natural judge.

2. Hypothetical dispute between the Community and a non-member State

The real difficulty arising from the incompatibility of an agreement concluded between a Member State and a non-member State with an agreement concluded by the Community has still to be faced.

The result of the above judgments handed down by the Court of Justice of the European Communities is that while the Community must not impede the implementation by a Member State of an agreement covered by Article 234, it is completely free to conclude an agreement on the same subject. Such an agreement might partially or wholly nullify the effects of the previous agreement.

In the cases which have so far arisen, the Community's position has been made easier by the fact that it had to deal with an individual who was not a citizen of a Community country but came under the courts of a Member State by virtue of territorial competence and, therefore, within the competence of the Court of Justice of the European Communities. In practice, Spain which already had an agreed relationship with the Community had no interest in taking action for its citizen. Had Spain done so its legal position would have been difficult because it would apparently have been accepting

---

[1] Judgment of 8.12.1981, Case 181/80 *Arbelaiz Emazabel* [1981] ECR 2961; judgment of 8.12.1981, Joined Cases 180 and 266/80 *Toma and Yurrita* [1981] ECR 2997. See note by Ch. Philip, Annuaire français de droit international, 1981, pp. 322-329; judgment of 28.10.1982, Joined Cases 138 and 139/81 *Marticorena-Otazo and Prego Parada* [1982] ECR 3819; judgment of 28.10.1982, Joined Cases 137 and 140/81 *Campandeguy Sagarzazu and Echeverria Sagasti* [1982] ECR 3847.

that agreements concluded with Member States should be replaced by an agreement concluded with the Community.[1]

It can even be held that if the Court had accepted the theory that the Communities had succeeded to rights and obligations resulting from agreements concluded by Member States, it might have concluded that the provisions of the earlier agreements were inapplicable on the principle that *lex posterior derogat priori* (later law cancels previous law), the agreements then being deemed to involve the same parties, namely the Member State on the one hand and the Community on the other in all cases.

The situation could arise, however, in which the Communities would one day have to answer a complaint from a non-member State arguing that a Community agreement concluded with another non-member State prevented a Member State from properly implementing an agreement concluded with it (the complainant).

In that hypothetical case, the body deciding the issue (which would not be the Court of Justice of the European Communities unless the case were referred to it by international compromise) would have no reason to argue the precedence of Community law. It takes precedence within the Community system but not outside.

The tribunal settling the case would then have to rule on the basis of the general rules of international law and would have to determine to what extent the existence of the Community agreement could constitute legitimate grounds for the total or partial abrogation of the agreement concluded by the Member State with the non-member State.[2]

C – *Incompatibility between a Community agreement and a subsequent agreement concluded between a Member State and a non-member State*

This question has to be considered from the standpoint of Community law and from the international standpoint.

Under the terms of paragraph 1 of Article 5 of the EEC Treaty the conclusion by a Member State of an agreement incompatible with Community law (which includes

---

[1] Apart from the further fact that since the conclusion of the London Agreement, the content of the law of the sea has changed substantially, as the Court of Justice pointed out (paragraph 24 of the previously-quoted decision of 16.10.1980).

[2] The position of the non-member State might be strengthened by invoking the provisions of paragraph 1 of Article 234 of the EEC Treaty. It could claim that this provision is a genuine stipulation for others which third parties have the right to invoke on their own behalf.
It is true that, in accordance with treaty law, the existence of such a stipulation is not easy to establish because it has to be proved that the authors of the clause really 'intended' to confer a right on third parties. In the event, however, the Court rulings quoted, according to which the precise purpose of Article 234 is to safeguard the rights of third parties, might constitute an argument for such an interpretation.

agreements concluded by the Communities) constitutes an act contrary to that law, subject to the procedure for breach laid down in Article 169 of the same Treaty.

Under this procedure, the Court of Justice of the Communities does not have powers to annul an agreement concluded by a Member State. It can only rule that there has been a breach. It is then incumbent on the Member State to take the necessary measures, namely, it must terminate or modify the agreement to which it is party.

It should be noted that, if the issue arose, the accused Member State could argue that the agreement in question had been concluded by the Communities *ultra vires*. The Court of Justice would then have to rule on this point.

However that may be, any solutions adopted within the Community and implemented by the Member State concerned would have no authority over the non-member State. As stated earlier, the concept of the precedence of Community law quite clearly has no force outside the Community.

The Member State could not invoke Community law against the non-member State as binding grounds for abrogating the agreement. The non-member State could then sue the Member State for breach of an international undertaking.

Section 2: Implementation of Community agreements under Community 'internal law' and under the law of Member States

According to the old view of international law, international agreements were deemed to apply to international relations only, that is to consitute the basis for an exchange of undertakings involving only subjects of international law.

This situation has now completely ceased to exist. Today, international agreements very often affect the legal system of States, and thereby change the rights and obligations of subjects of internal law in relation to the legal order. This applies most particularly in the case of 'economic' agreements.

On the issue of the relationship between internal law and the execution of treaties, international law has only one rule, namely that internal law cannot be invoked as grounds for failing to implement an agreement, should the case arise.[1]

But this rule applies only to international implementation of the agreement. In practice, only a party to the agreement – and hence a subject of international law – can, should the case arise, argue failure to implement against the other party.

---

[1] Subject, as will be shown later, to a defect affecting consent given to the agreement.

On the other hand, the question of the internal implementation of the agreement can be raised by subjects of internal law, who demand that rights which they claim to enjoy under the agreement shall be applied to their benefit.

The issue is then referred to the internal law institutions – the executive and the courts.

There is, of course, nothing to prevent a State from taking up the case of one of its nationals and claiming that the failure of the other party to implement a treaty properly in its own country constitutes a breach of international contractual obligations on its part.

However, in the present state of international law, such an action would only have a chance of succeeding if the inadequate internal execution or implementation amounted to a denial of justice, that is a gross breach of the basic guarantees to which foreign nationals are entitled.

However, the fact of according a law precedence over a previous treaty or of declaring that a provision of an agreement 'cannot be invoked' does not of itself constitute a denial of justice, as the citizen concerned has been able to use a normal, non-discriminatory legal procedure.

The issue of the internal implementation of the agreement is therefore separate in fact from that of its international implementation.

As regards the internal implementation of an international agreement, the problem identified in respect of States can be transposed to the Communities.

It will first be recalled that the Court of Justice of the European Communities ruled that an agreement binding on the Communities is an integral part of Community law.

The next point to consider is whether Community practice is 'monistic' or 'dualistic', what position an agreement occupies in the hierarchy of sources of Community law and to what extent the terms of an agreement can be invoked by individuals (self-executing effect).

A – Community agreements, integral part
of Community law

When called on to consider an interlocutory question regarding the interpretation of a provision of the association agreement concluded between the Community and Greece, the Court took the view that the agreement in question formed an integral part of Community law and was within its competence, specifically under Article 177.[1]

---

[1] Judgment of 30.4.1974, Case 181/73 *Haegeman* [1974] ECR 449.

This decision is of considerable significance, because it establishes the Court of Justice as the authority on the interpretation and application of Community agreements, in relation to national courts which in the natural order of things hear complaints from individuals regarding the 'internal' execution of an international agreement.

This rule applies to 'Community' agreements, that is agreements to which the Community is party, including joint agreements which associate the Community and Member States.[1] It also applies to agreements to which the Community has become 'party', not by the normal way of conclusion but by 'succession', limited so far to the case of the GATT.[2]

It does not apply, however, to agreements to which only the Member States are parties, even if they have a link with the Community system (agreements covered by Article 220 of the EEC Treaty).

B – Application of 'monism' to Community agreements

Doctrinal arguments on the respective reality and value of the monist and dualist systems are innumerable.

There are of course many variants of both systems.

In our view, however, there is one indisputable criterion for distinguishing between them.

Dualism applies when, in the legal system in question, an international agreement cannot, as such, constitute a source of rights and obligations. Only an instrument of internal law can do so, when it is adopted in connection with the agreement and when it introduces, executes, implements or refers to the agreement.[3]

Symmetrically, monism applies when it is accepted that an international agreement *can* as such constitute a source of rights and obligations. The mere formality of publishing the agreement – which is followed in all the major legal systems including that of the Community – does not constitute a procedure for introducing the agreement into internal law insofar as it applies to the agreement in the same way as it applies to any legal instrument which can be invoked against third parties. Consequently, the fact that an agreement can only become applicable in internal law from the date of publication does not imply a dualist option. Quite on the contrary, if the only internal legal procedure

---

[1] Judgment of 5.2.1976, Case 87/75 *Bresciani* [1976] ECR 121.
[2] Judgment of 12.12.1972, Joined Cases 21 to 24/72, *International Fruit,* previously mentioned; judgment of 19.11.1975, Case 38/75, *Nederlandse Spoorwegen,* previously mentioned; judgment of 16.3.1983, Joined Cases 266 and 267/81 [1983] ECR 801 *et seq.*
[3] K.M. Meessen, *'The application of rules of public international law within Community law',* Common Market Law Review, 1976, pp. 489-501.

applying to agreements is that of publication, the *a priori* conclusion is that the system is monist.

Arguments as to whether the Community system is monist or dualist have been obscured by overlooking the essential criterion for differentiation and by taking too much account of the procedures used by the Community for the conclusion of agreements.

Community acceptance is published in the *Official Journal of the European Communities,* usually as an annex to a 'Council decision concluding . . .'.[1]

Agreement may also be annexed to a 'Council Regulation concerning the conclusion of. . .'[2]

The fact that two procedures are used has given rise to the hypothesis that regulations have to be used in the case of agreements conferring rights on individuals but that decisions apply to agreements limited to an exchange of 'international' undertakings.

Starting from that premise, the dualist argument has been able to maintain that an agreement not published by regulation could not be such as to confer rights on individuals.

Similarly, it has been noted that when the courts of a dualist State refer to the Court of Justice for a ruling on the direct enforceability of a treaty, they are often careful to refer to the Community instrument used for publication, at least when a regulation is involved.[3]

In our view, however, it cannot be claimed solely on the basis of a single case and episode that the Community applies a dualist system.

Firstly, there are no grounds for maintaining that a regulation has greater force than a decision in creating rights. Exactly like a regulation, a decision is intended to create rights and obligations, the only criterion for distinction being whether or not the measure is of general application.

Secondly, the introduction or transformation of an international rule into an internal rule is not the same as the question of the creation of rights for individuals. In monist

---

[1] See for example: Council Decision of 25.6.1974 concluding the International Wheat Agreement of 1971 (OJ L 219, 1974). Council Decision of 3.3.1975 concluding the Convention on the prevention of marine pollution from land-based sources (OJ L 194, 1975). Council Decision of 26.9.1983 concerning notification of the provisional application by the EEC of the 1983 International Coffee Agreement (OJ L 308, 1983).

[2] For example, Council Regulation of 3.6.1977 concerning conclusion of the agreement between the EEC and the government of the United States of America concerning fishing in the United States off-shore waters (OJ L 161, 1977).

[3] For example, in the *Polydor* case, the Court of Appeal of England and Wales framed its question as follows: 'Is Article 14(2) of the said Agreement (EEC-Portugal) dated 22 July 1980 directly enforceable by individuals within the EEC having regard in particular to the said EEC Council regulation dated 19 December 1972 giving effect to the said Agreement?'. (See judgment of 9.2.1982, Case 270/80, [1982] ECR 329.)

systems, every agreement is not deemed *ipso facto* to create rights. It has to be interpreted to establish whether this is the case.

Thirdly, and in any event, it is not for the executive to choose between monism and dualism. In all legal systems, it is normally the courts which, when ruling on the rights claimed by an individual under an agreement, have to decide in favour of monism or dualism, in accordance with the constitution. The Court of Justice of the European Communities took the view that an agreement was 'an integral part of Community law' without referring to any procedure for transformation or introduction but solely to its entry into force.[1]

It further took the view that agreements could create rights for individuals without considering the instrument of Community law which had approved and published the agreements.[2]

Similarly, arguing by implication in the cases relating to the GATT, the Court did not consider that the absence of any procedure for introduction of that agreement into Community law – and with good reason because it had not been 'concluded' by the Community – was grounds for ruling that the agreement could not be invoked directly. It was on another basis – the interpretation of the agreement itself – that the Court ruled, in that case, that the provisions in question could not be invoked.

It should therefore be very firmly concluded that, under the Community system, an agreement is enforceable in internal law by virtue of the sole fact that it has entered into force and been published without having to refer to the concept of introduction of the agreement into Community law.[3]

It should be added that the monist system does not of cource prohibit the adoption of internal provisions for implementing an agreement.

This may be necessary when the agreement in question is imprecise or simply provides an outline reference.

The decisions to implement then have separate value, but they do not affect the internal scope of the agreement as such.

C – *Position of the agreement in the hierarchy of sources*

The position of the agreement in the hierarchy of sources of internal law does not depend entirely on application of the dualist or the monist system.

---

[1] Judgment of 30.4.1974, Case 181/73, *Haegeman,* previously quoted.

[2] See in particular judgment of 5.2.1976, Case 87/75, previously quoted, especially paragraphs 16 to 18.

[3] The fact that an agreement is an 'integral part' of Community law means that it becomes subject to all the principles which apply to Community law. Consequently, monism must also apply in relation to Member States in regard to such agreements, because they participate in their enforcement. The Court of Justice in fact excluded any formality for 'acceptance' or order for enforcement of Community law in internal law.

In a dualist system, the hierarchical status of the agreement is, of course, determined by the nature of the rule of internal law by which it is introduced. The question is therefore resolved.

By contrast, in a monist system, the absence of any machinery for introduction does not mean that the agreement must of necessity take precedence over or yield precedence to a particular rule of internal law.

The place of an agreement is fixed by the constitution and (or) by court rulings. In France, for example, the constitution provides that 'treaties or agreements duly ratified or approved take precedence over laws, from the time of their publication provided each agreement or treaty is enforced by the other party' (Article 55). In practice, however, the precedence of an agreement over legislation – when subsequent – has not yet been fully established, because the French administrative courts have refused to rule against laws contrary to agreements.

The hierarchical position of agreements among Community sources is not fully defined by the Treaties establishing the Communities.

Under the terms of paragraphs 2 and 3 of Article 228 of the EEC Treaty, an agreement declared by the Court to be incompatible with this Treaty can only enter into force after the said Treaty has been amended.

From this it must be deduced that agreements are subordinate to the establishing Treaties.

While this solution is completely logical – not only because it is the one currently applied in various ways in the national systems, but also because it also respects the principle that the European Communities are a 'special case' – it cannot be accepted that the Community institutions are allowed to exceed their powers by way of an international agreement, when they cannot do so by way of a unilateral instrument.

Furthermore, Article 235 acts as a safety valve when necessary, because it allows the Community to conclude agreements in order to attain any of its objectives.[1] If, therefore, the EEC wishes to conclude an agreement which exceeds its powers in the strict sense, it simply has to make use of Article 235.

The establishing Treaties did not, however, determine the position of agreements in relation to unilateral Community instruments.

The Court of Justice of the European Communities has, however, ruled that agreements take precedence over derived law.[2]

---

[1] J. Raux, 'Le recours à l'Article 235 du traité CEE en vue de la conclusion d'accords externes, Mélanges en l'honneur de P.H. Teitgen, Pedone, 1984, pp. 407-439.

[2] Previously-mentioned judgments in the *International Fruit* and *Haegeman* cases.

Any previous or subsequent unilateral Community instrument, contrary to a Community instrument, is therefore invalid. The Court also allowed the right to sue for breach of a Community agreement.[1]

D – Right to invoke agreements as grounds for legal action

The use of obscure or unsuitable formulae, such as 'self-executing', or 'immediately' or 'directly' enforceable and the assimilation of this question to the distinction between monism and dualism, have not helped the question to be stated in clear terms.

The issue, as clearly indicated by the Court of Justice, is whether the provisions of a Community agreement can 'create for anyone subject to Community law the right to rely on such agreements before the courts' in order to contest the validity of a Community instrument[2] or of a national measure.[3]

This is why the expression 'invocability of agreements' presents the problem correctly.

In this context, it is usual to refer to the ruling given by the Permanent International Court of Justice on 3 March 1928 in the case concerning the competence of Dantzig courts. The Court ruled that the purpose of a treaty was normally to produce international and not internal effects. It accepted, however, that it might be the intention of the parties that a treaty should produce internal effects.[4] These would therefore constitute an exception.

This isolated opinion could not of itself establish a customary rule. Furthermore, it was given at a time when very few international treaties were capable of having an effect in internal law.

It nevertheless showed that the only acceptable way of answering the question put was by interpretation of the agreement.

This was confirmed by the practice of domestic courts, which also revealed the variety of the criteria used for interpretation.

---

[1] Judgment of 30.4.1974, Case 181/73, *Haegeman,* previously mentioned.

[2] Judgment of 24.10.1973, Case 9/73, *Schluter,* previously mentioned (paragraph 28). Similarly in the previously-mentioned judgment given in *International Fruit* case: 'In order that the incompatibility of a Community instrument with a provision of international law shall affect the validity of that instrument, the Community must first be bound by the said provision. In the event that invalidity is claimed before a national court, it is also necessary that the said provision shall be such as to create for persons subject to Community law the right to rely on that provision before the courts'. On the other hand, when referring to invocability, the Court used the much less satisfactory expression 'directly enforceable', but immediately added that this referred to the problem of invocability in the *Pabst* case (Case 17/81, 25.4.1982, paragraphs 27 and 28, [1982] ECR 1331). The same applied in the *Kupferberg* case (Case 104/81, 26.10.1982, [1982] ECR 2364).

[3] *Bresciani* case, previously mentioned, paragraph 16.

[4] PICJ Series B, No 15, p. 17.

Far from confining themselves to trying to establish what the parties intended, the courts – which increasingly recognize the existence of provisions which can be invoked – mostly prefer to base themselves on an objective interpretation which mainly analyses the general characteristics of the treaty and the individual characteristics of the provision in question.[1]

Before considering the solutions adopted by the Community in the matter, it has to be stated that the question of the invocability of a treaty provision is not to be confused with that of the application of a monist or a dualist system.

In monist States, the courts do not accept the presumption that the provisions of international agreements can be invoked but decide case by case. This is clearly the position with the French courts, for example.

In dualist States, while it is true that an international agreement can never be deemed to be a source of rights and obligations and cannot therefore be 'invoked' before the courts, the existence of an internal provision which transforms or introduces the agreements does not have the indirect effect of entitling individuals to invoke all the provisions of the agreement.

Thus, the German Constitutional Court took the view that 'only the provisions of international agreements possessing all the characteristics which an internal law must possess in order to create rights or obligations can be transformed, by the approving law into law enforceable within the internal legal system; a provision of an international treaty must, by virtue of its text, be objective and the content be of such nature as to entail legal effects on the same basis as a provision of internal law. It is on this condition only that legal rules binding on citizens can be created'.[2]

In other words, dualism does not eliminate the need to interpret an agreement in order to determine whether it contains provisions which may be 'invoked'. The interpretation may of course be given by the authority which has to adopt the introducing order; but this interpretation may be reviewed by the courts, under the German system at least.

---

[1] The French courts very often rule by implication on the question of a direct right to invoke without stating criteria. It is found that the judge took the view that the treaty could be invoked directly because he had given full consideration to the argument based on the contradiction between the agreement and the internal provision attacked (for example, Conseil d'État, 20.5.1977; Syndicat national d'infirmiers et infirmières diplômés d'État, CER, p. 225). The stated grounds for refusing the right to invoke are usually that the agreement could only create obligations between the States parties (for example Cass. Civ., 6.4.1976, Fauran Journal de droit international, 1976, p. 903).
Conversely, the ruling handed down by the Swiss Federal Court on 13.10.1972, Banque de Crédit international versus Conseil d'État of Geneva Canton (*Cahier de droit européen*, 1974, 181) can be quoted as an example of a judgment giving detailed grounds for a direct right to invoke an agreement. On American court rulings see S.A. Riesenfeld, *'The doctrine of self-executing treaties and US'* and *'US v Postal: Win at any price?'* American Journal of International Law, 1980, Vol. 74, pp. 892-904.
[2] Ruling of 9.12.1970, cited in *Fontes juris gentium*, A II, Vol. 6, pp. 9/27.

Within the Community, full extent of the question of the right to invoke a Community agreement – although considered by the Court as long ago as 1972 – was not appreciated at the outset.

Chronologically, the Court first handed down two decisions on the subject, both concerning the GATT.[1]

The Court next ruled on the right to invoke the provisions of the Yaoundé Convention.[2]

More recently, the Court had to consider almost at the same time – in all cases by way of preliminary question – whether it was possible to invoke directly Articles 14 and 23 of the agreement between the EEC and Portugal;[3] Article 53(1) of the agreement of association between the EEC and Greece;[4] Article 21(1) of the agreement between the EEC and Portugal.[5]

The governments of Member States and the Commission attached great importance to these cases and tabled very detailed comments. In the *Polydor* case, the Court did not deem it necessary to answer the question regarding direct invocability. It did so briefly in the *Pabst* case. Lastly, in the *Kupferberg* case, it went into very detailed arguments as it wished to state its decision as a principle.[6]

Scrutiny of all these rulings shows that the Court refined its methods of interpretation between *International Fruit* and *Kupferberg*.

In the two cases concerning the GATT, the Court after having stated that 'the spirit, economy and terms of the General Agreement must all be taken into account' confined itself to an overall interpretation of the agreement to deduce that 'set in that context', the article in question was not such as to create for justiciable persons the right to invoke it in a court of law.

In the *Bresciani* case, the Court repeated the formulae used in earlier cases, but went on not only to interpret the convention as such but also to analyse the provision in ques-

---

[1] Judgment of 12.12.1972, Joined Cases 21 to 24/72 *International Fruit,* and judgment of 24.10.1973, Case 9/73, *Schluter,* previously mentioned. The Court referred to the grounds for its decision in the *International Fruit* case in its judgments of 16.3.1983, Cases 266, 267 to 269/81, *SIOT, SPI, SAMI,* previously mentioned.

[2] Judgment of 5.2.1976, Case 87/75, *Bresciani,* previously mentioned.

[3] Judgment of 9.2.1982, Case 270/80, *Polydor,* previously mentioned.

[4] Judgment of 29.4.1982, Case 17/81, *Pabst,* previously mentioned.

[5] Judgment of 26.10.1982, Case 104/81, *Kupferberg,* previously mentioned.

[6] The most recent studies on the subject are:
(i) G. Bebr, *'Agreements concluded by the Community and their possible direct effect: from International Fruit to Kupferberg',* Common Market Law Review, 20, 1983, pp. 35-73;
(ii) P.J. Choffat, *'L'applicabilité directe de l'accord de libre-échange du 22 juillet 1972 entre la CEE et la Confédération Suisse',* (Thesis, Lausanne, 1977);
(iii) J. Groux, *'L'"invocabilité" en justice des accords internationaux des Communautés européennes, à propos de plusieurs arrêts récents de la CJCE',* Rev. trim. de droit européen, 1983, pp. 3-32;
(iv) H.G. Schermers, *'The direct application of treaties with third States: note concerning the Polydor and Pabst cases',* Common Market Law Review, 19, 1982, pp. 563-569.

tion set in its 'context' and concluded that Article 2(1) of the convention which required the Community to abolish taxes of equivalent effect in relation to the associated States 'was precise and not subject to any implicit or explicit reservations on the part of the Community and was therefore such as to create for justiciable persons the right to avail themselves of it before the courts'.

In the *Pabst* case, the Court, after briefly restating the context, similarly took the view that Article 53(1) of the agreement 'involved a clear and precise obligation, the execution and effects of which are not subordinate to the intervention of any subsequent instrument'.

The *Kupferberg* decision is in line with the two previous ones, because the Court took account of the characteristics of both the agreement and the relevant provision.

Its analysis was more complex, however, because it was in three stages and not two.

The first stage was scrutiny of the agreement as a whole in order to determine that 'neither the nature nor the economy of the agreement (could) prevent an economic operator from invoking one of the provisions of the said agreement before a Community court'.

The second stage was to set the relevant provision in its context in order to determine its exact purpose and scope.

The third stage was the interpretation of the provision. The conclusion was that the obligation stipulated was 'unconditional and sufficently precise' to be invoked by individuals.

In conclusion, on the basis of the Court's reasoning, it can be affirmed that a provision of an agreement can be invoked before a court, except if it results from its text or context that the alleged obligation is conditional or imprecise or if – notwithstanding the content of the provision – the general characteristics of the agreement in any way create an obstacle to its being invoked before the courts.

The *Kupferberg* decision went further than a refinement of the Court's method of interpretation. It also allowed the Court to state its position on the arguments submitted by the governments of several Member States, the Commission and the Advocate General in the *Polydor* case, seeking to dissuade the Court from accepting too easily that the provision of an agreement could be invoked.[1]

---

[1] In the *Polydor* case four of the five governments intervening, the Commission and the Advocate General concluded that the provisions in question could not be invoked.

In the *Kupferberg* case, the three intervening governments maintained that the agreement could not be invoked, as did the Advocate General.

The Commission, in more cautious and carefully-phrased terms, proposed that Article 21(1) of the EEC-Portugal agreement should be deemed invocable by virtue of a substantive interpretation of the said article whereby its scope would be less than that of Article 95(1) of the EEC Treaty.

On the other hand, the Commission concluded that Article 21(1) could not be invoked if the Court recognized it to have the same scope as Article 95(1). In other words, the Commission linked recognition of the right to invoke to the substantive interpretation of the provision.

These arguments were as follows:

(i) It would be inopportune and probably imprudent to transfer almost automatically to international agreements concluded by the Community the criteria which enabled the Court to determine that the provisions of the Community Treaties and of law derived therefrom could be invoked.

(ii) The powers of the Court to interpret the Community's international agreements would be such as to affect the balance of the Community's institutions, in particular if the effect were to transfer to the Court powers held by the parties to the agreement.

(iii) In ruling on direct invocability of an agreement, the Court should take account of the problem of reciprocity and should consider whether recognition of invocability within the Community might not put the Community at a disadvantage as compared with partners who do not recognize such invocability.[1]

The Court made no explicit ruling on the first point. It can however be deduced from its manner of proceeding – and also from its earlier decisions – that it does not consider itself in any way bound by the criteria which it used to determine whether Community law in the strict sense could be invoked in respect of persons subject to it.[2]

Regarding the second argument – based on the fact that agreements are an integral part of the Community legal system – the Court formally restated its exclusive right of interpretation because 'it could not be accepted that their effects within the Community should vary according to whether they are to be interpreted, in practice, by the Community institutions or by the Member States and, in the latter case, according to the attitude taken in law in each of the Member States in respect of the effects produced, within their internal order, by international agreements concluded by them'.[3]

At the same time it declared its respect for the independence of the parties' wishes by stating:

'In accordance with the principles of international law, the Community institutions which have powers to negotiate and conclude an agreement with a non-member country are at liberty to agree with that country the effects which the provisions of that agreement are to have within the internal order of the contracting parties. It is only

---

[1] The Advocate General, Mrs Rozès, was very specific on this point and argued that 'To recognize that a provision of this agreement is of direct effect without any guarantee that an individual can invoke that provision in Portugal on the same terms and conditons and with the same consequences in respect of legal protection would, because of the absence of reciprocity, ultimately be to the disadvantage of the Community, which was not the intention of the contracting parties so far as it can be determined (...)'.

[2] In the *Bresciani* case, Advocate General Trabucchi took this position ([1975] ECR 149). In the *Bouhelier* case, the Court rejected in clear terms the thesis that arguments applied to intra-Community relationships could be transposed to extra-Community relationships (11.10.1979, [1979] ECR 315).

In the *Polydor* case in particular, the Court clearly stated (paragraphs 14, 15, 16, 17, 18), that the fact that the wording of provisions of the EEC Treaty was identical with that of a trade agreement concluded between the EEC and a non-member country was not sufficient grounds for transposing to the interpretation of that agreement the elements and criteria used by the Court in respect of the EEC Treaty itself.

[3] *Kupferberg* judgment: paragraph 14.

when this question has not been settled by the agreement that it has to be resolved by the competent courts and in particular the Court ... on the same basis as all other questions relating to the interpretation of the agreement within the Community'.[1]

Lastly, the Court categorically rejected the third argument, which was probably the most important, in the following terms:

'In accordance with the general rules of international law, every agreement must be enforced in good faith by the parties. Each of the contracting parties is responsible for the full implementation of the commitments it has entered into, but has to determine the appropriate legal means of achieving that purpose within its own legal system, unless the agreement, interpreted in the light of its aim and objective, itself determines the appropriate means.

Subject to this final proviso, the fact that the courts in one of the parties consider that some of the provisions of the agreement are directly enforceable, while the courts of the other party do not accept such direct enforceability, is not of itself and alone such as to consitute non-reciprocity in the implementation of the agreement'.[2]

Finally, it may be considered that the Community legal system now accepts a much fuller theory of the direct invocability of agreements than do many national legal systems.

This theory cannot of course immediately remove all uncertainty for justiciable subjects because the text always has to be interpreted.

It has, however, the merit of determining the essential stages in the argument to be followed.

Section 3: Community powers and nullity of agreements

Although practice in this area is very limited, it is accepted that an international agreement can cease to exist when grounds for nullity supervene.

Such causes may first of all be defects affecting the consent given to the agreement by one or more parties as, for example, the body giving consent being unqualified to do so, error, corruption or constraint. It may also be a case of incompatibility between one or more provisions of the agreement and a superior rule of international law (*jus cogens* rule).

---

[1] Paragraph 17.
[2] Paragraph 18.

The theory of the nullity of agreements, worked out in great detail in the Vienna Convention on the Law of Treaties, applies to agreements to which international organizations are parties. This theory is simply transposed to the previously-mentioned ILC project on this point.

However, in the case of international organizations there remains the difficult specific problem of agreements concluded by an organization *ultra vires.*

States normally have plenary powers in the matter of international relations, but international organizations are governed by the principle of 'special character'.

On this point, the ILC project takes a middle course – already adopted in the Vienna Convention on treaty law as regards State bodies unqualified to conclude a treaty – and considers that an international organization cannot claim that its consent to be bound by an agreement was expressed in violation of the rules concerning powers to conclude treaties 'unless such violation was manifest and concerns a fundamentally-important rule of its internal law'.[1]

In the absence of any practice in the matter, such a provision cannot be deemed to codify the existing law. It is not out of the question, however, that it might serve as a reference in case of dispute.

Although the question has never yet arisen, there is no doubt that the European Communities could be confronted, at some stage, with the problem of an agreement which they had concluded *ultra vires.*

The question is the more serious because Community law provides for legal procedures for the punishment of any breach of the establishing rules and therefore any *ultra vires* action.

Admittedly, this risk is very minor because the EEC Treaty provides for 'preventive' monitoring by the procedure laid down in Article 228, paragraph 2.

The paragraph reads: 'The Council, the Commission or a Member State may obtain beforehand the opinion of the Court of Justice as to whether an agreement envisaged is compatible with the provisions of this Treaty. Where the opinion of the Court of Justice is adverse the agreement may enter into force only in accordance with Article 236'.[2]

However, the existence of this procedure in no way excludes the subsequent condemnation of an agreement concluded contrary to certain provisions of the establishing Treaties.

---

[1] Article 46.3 of the project. Paragraph 4 specifies that 'A violation is manifest if it is known or should be known to every contracting State or organization'.

[2] In the first decision under this procedure (Opinion 1/75, previously mentioned) the Court of Justice ruled that 'the compatibility of an agreement with the provisions of the Treaty must be assessed in the light of all the rules of the Treaty, including, that is, the rules which determine the extent of the Community institutions' powers as well as the fundamental rules'.

In its 1975 opinion the Court of Justice was at pains to stress that 'the question whether the conclusion of a given agreement is or is not within the powers of the Community and whether, in the specific case, those powers have been exercised in accordance with the provisions of the Treaty (are) normally referable to the Court of Justice either directly under Article 169 or Article 173 of the Treaty or by the preliminary procedure'.

Although the Court stressed immediately before this ruling that the condemnation of a treaty already in force would create a difficult situation, the possibility cannot be excluded that a treaty concluded by the Community may be declared null and void or invalid by the Court of Justice.[1]

The Community would then find itself in the same position as a State, one of whose competent courts had declared a treaty to be unconstitutional and therefore null and void or invalid.[2]

A decision by a 'domestic' court has, of course, no direct effect in international law. The treaty therefore continues in being.

On the other hand, it requires the executive to cease enforcing the agreements or the part thereof which has been ruled to be contrary to a higher rule of internal law.

The Community would therefore be in the position of not enforcing an agreement and might be sued internationally.

Assuming that the rules proposed by the ILC and discussed earlier achieve the authority of a rule of international law, it might be possible to argue that the breach of a rule regarding competence had been manifest and concerned a 'rule of fundamental importance'. In that case, the Community could lawfully rely on the initial defect as an argument against the other contracting parties and could claim that the defect was so patent that they could not be unaware of it.

It has to be admitted, however, that the assumption of a treaty concluded by the Community 'manifestly' *ultra vires* is a highly unlikely one.[3]

---

[1] 'A court ruling that such an agreement is, by virtue either of its content or of the procedure by which it was concluded, incompatible with the provisions of the Treaty must inevitably create serious difficulties both for the Community and for international relations and could be prejudicial to all interested parties, including non-member countries'.

[2] This is not possible under all the legal systems. A Netherlands court cannot do so, for example.

[3] The Court also monitors the joint agreements.

It can therefore rule against any sharing of powers, within an agreement, between the Community and the Member States, if it considers such sharing to be contrary to Community law.

Such a Court decision should lead the Community and the Member States to amend the agreement but not normally in such manner as to affect the implementation of the agreement in regard to third parties.

Section 4: Implementation of Community agreements by Member States

In accordance with the principles of the relative effect of treaties, only parties thereto are bound by an agreement and therefore responsible for its enforcement.

This principle is less clear if the 'non-member States' are in fact the member States of an organization in the case of an agreement concluded by that organization.

It would appear logical at first sight to provide that the member States are bound by the provisions of the agreement if it is considered that the 'consent' of the organization is simply 'derived' from that of the States.

But the States have little enthusiasm for this solution under which they are responsible, financially as well as otherwise, for any agreement concluded by an organization.

The difficulty is clearly illustrated by the discussions which took place in the International Law Commission when a project on the subject was being drafted.

This project was redrafted several times with substantial variations. It appeared to be accepted from the outset that, as a general rule, the member States of an organization were not bound by organization agreements to which they were parties. Further restrictive amendments were made to a first draft, stipulating that this was not so when the organization's establishing texts made such provision.[1]

It is clear therefore that the general tendency, as reflected in the ILC draft, is towards the separation of the organization from its member States.

The EEC does not conform to this general tendency in any way.

---

[1] Present text:
'The member States of an international organization acquire obligations and rights under the provisions of a treaty to which that organization is party when the parties to that agreement agree, by those provisions to create such obligations and confer such rights and have defined their conditions and effects in that treaty or have otherwise agreed, and if:
(a) the member States of the organization have unanimously agreed to be bound by the said provisions of the treaty, by virtue of the instrument establishing that organization or in some other manner; and
(b) the consent of the member States of the organization to be bound by relevant provisions of the treaty has been duly notified to the States and organizations which have taken part in the negotiations'.
The first draft of this article was both simpler and less restrictive, namely:
'Third States which are members of an organization should fulfil the obligations and may exercise the rights created for them by the provisions of a treaty to which the organization is party if:
(a) the relevant rules of the organization in force at the time of implementation of the treaty provide that the member States of the organization are bound by the treaty concluded by the latter; or if
(b) the States and organizations taking part in the negotiation of the treaty and the member States of the organization have agreed that the execution of the treaty necessarily involves those effects'.
Cf. Ph. Manin, 'L'article 228, alinéa 2, du traité CEE', in Mélanges en l'honneur de P.H. Teitgen, Pedone, Paris, 1984, pp.289-310.

The EEC Treaty in fact contains Article 228, paragraph 2, which provides: 'Agreements concluded under these conditions shall be binding on the institutions of the Community and on Member States.'

By virtue of the principle of the unity of the legal person in relation to the rest of the world, all institutions of the State or organization are required to enforce the agreement, each insofar as it is concerned.[1] The provision that 'institutions' are bound therefore adds nothing to the accepted customary rules.

On the other hand, the declaration that the Member States are also bound clearly goes beyond those rules.

The importance of Article 228(2) was highlighted by the decision given by the Court of Justice in the *Kupferberg* case, in the following terms:

'Under the terms of paragraph 2 of Article 228, the Member States are bound by these agreements *in the same way* [our emphasis] as the said institutions. In consequence, both the Community institutions and the Member States are required to ensure compliance with the obligations created by such agreements.

In ensuring the fulfilment of undertakings resulting from an agreement concluded by the Community institutions, the Member States fulfil an obligation not only in relation to the non-member countries concerned but also and most importantly towards the Community, which has assumed responsibility for the proper enforcement of the agreement. As the Court previously ruled on 30 April 1974 (Haegeman), the provisions of such an agreement form an integral part of the Community's legal system'.[2]

The interest of these arguments does not lie primarily in the obligation on Member States to enforce the agreement in relation to the Community.

There can be no doubt that since Community agreements have been deemed to be 'an integral part of the Community legal system', the Member States have the same duties – and are subject to the same penalties in case of non-execution – as in the case of a regulation, for example.

It is important, on the other hand, that the Court stated, even if only incidentally, that the Member States are fulfilling an obligation towards the non-member countries concerned, under the terms of paragraph 2 of Article 228.

---

[1] In order to be binding on both institutions and States, the agreements must have been concluded 'under the conditions laid down' in paragraph 1 of Article 228.
It should be deduced from this that an agreement concluded under conditions contrary to the rule (in form or substance) is not binding. But in view of the principle that no-one can be judge in his own case within the Community, the decision has to be made by the Court of Justice. Until such time as an agreement has been annulled or declared invalid by the Court it continues to be binding and to be enforced.
In strict law, if the restrictive proviso concerning 'conditions laid down' had not been included, it may be questioned to what extent the Court of Justice would be entitled to annul or declare invalid an irregularly concluded agreement because as an 'institution' it would be required to enforce the agreement in accordance with Article 228, paragraph 2.
[2] Paragraphs 11 and 13 of the *Kupferberg* judgment.

The likely consequences as regards responsibility will be considered later.[1]

It remains to consider whether and how the foregoing reasoning and conclusions are modified in the case of a mixed agreement.

In our view, the answer depends on the type of mixed agreement.

In the case of such an agreement which does not include a 'list of powers' or does not explicitly enumerate in its provisions the obligations devolving upon the Community and those devolving on the Member States, the division of powers between the Community and its Member States cannot be invoked against third parties.

Third parties can, as they choose, call upon either the Community or its Member States to implement any part of the agreement. The difference as compared with a 'Community' agreement lies in the fact that in this case the contracting parties can take action directly against the Member States because they are parties to the agreement.

By contrast, if the mixed agreement clearly indentifies what devolves upon the Community and what devolves upon the Member States or – even more so – if it includes a list enumerating the respective powers of each, notified to the contracting parties, the situation becomes less clear.

While it may be regarded as certain that a contracting party cannot call on the Member States to execute in due form the Community part of the agreement, it may be asked whether that party can call on the Community to require proper execution of the agreement by the Member States. On the basis of Article 228(2), it should be able to do this for the 'Community part' of the agreement, but not for the non-Community parts. Or more accurately, the Community could in that case declare the demand to be inadmissible.

This shows clearly that far from adding to their safeguards, the list of powers which non-member countries sometimes request would rather tend to reduce them.

However that may be, it is apparent that the Community system differs radically from the general system.

In the case of international agreements concluded by the Community it creates a joint responsibility between the Community and its Member States which, at first sight, looks to be to the advantage of non-member countries, because it strengthens, if necessary, the guarantees that the agreement will be implemented.

---

[1] See Chapter II below, p. 14.

Section 5: Grounds claimed by the Communities for the suspension or abrogation of an agreement

Every international agreement should be implemented in good faith. Withdrawal from an agreement to which one is party without being able to produce legitimate grounds is an act for which its author is liable to be sued.

This is the intent of the rule expressed in the adage '*Pacta sunt servanda*' (agreements must be implemented).

This marks the difference between an international agreement proper and a political or gentlemen's agreement, from which one of the partners can withdraw for simple reasons of convenience.

There are a number of legitimate grounds on which one of the parties may cease to comply with an agreement to which it is party. Their use often leads to a dispute because if one of the parties considers that the conditions exist for suspension or abrogation, the other often disputes the fact. This is particularly the case when one of the parties claims a major infringement of the agreement by the other, a supervening situation which renders execution impossible or even a 'fundamental change of circumstances' *(rebus sic stantibus)*.

In addition to grounds for termination or suspension peculiar to an agreement, relations established by agreement between two or more subjects of international law can be affected by a global event.

For example, a state of war can be grounds for the suspension or termination of agreements between the belligerents.

Similarly, in the case of sanctions ordered by the United Nations Security Council on the basis of Article 41 of the charter (non-military sanctions), the Member States of the United Nations may be required to suspend the application of agreements with the State against which the sanctions are ordered, in order to apply those sanctions.

As parties to international agreements, the Communities could be in the position of having to invoke grounds for the termination or suspension of an agreement against the other contracting parties or of having such grounds invoked against themselves.

In the case of grounds internal to the agreement, the difficulties should be neither greater nor less than for agreements between States.

On the other hand, in the case of grounds for suspension or termination external to the agreement and associated with political events, the problem is complicated initially by the fact that it is the Member States which appear *a priori* to be directly concerned.

Thus, decisions of the Security Council are not addressed to the Communities because they are not members of the United Nations. Furthermore, Article 25 of the United Nations Charter specifies that Security Council resolutions are binding on *all member States of the United Nations.*

The Communities are not, therefore, directly bound by a Council decision; but the Member States are required to take the necessary measures to comply with the objectives stated in the decision and must, where appropriate, act to that end within the Community institutions.

In the discussion of precedents (South Africa and Southern Rhodesia), it was seen that the Member States insisted on taking the lead. [1]

By contrast, in other cases of 'sanctions' against a State considered to be responsible for an act contrary to international law, where the implementation of a United Nations decision was not involved, the Communities themselves took measures in areas within their jurisdiction. [2]

Special reference should be made to the Falkland Islands affair because a Member State was the direct victim of action by a non-member country and because hostilities took place between the two States without war being declared.

In this affair, the Communities considered themselves to be affected by the action taken by Argentina against the United Kingdom and acted accordingly. [3]

They did not, of course, have to consider the possibility of denouncing or suspending an agreement in force with the non-member State concerned.

If such had been the case and an international dispute had resulted, the question might have arisen as to whether the Communities can invoke a cause affecting one (or more) of their Member States as grounds for denouncing a 'Community' agreement.

It may be thought that they could do so under the terms of paragraph 2 of Article 228 which makes the Communities and their Member States jointly responsible for implementing Community agreements.

---

[1] See Part Two p. 96.

[2] Measures taken following the invasion of Afghanistan by Soviet forces, in respect of deliveries of agricultural products, food aid and special emergency aid for refugees (see Bulletin EC 1-1980, p. 9).
On the subject of trade sanctions against the USSR in response to events in Poland, see OJ, L 72 and OJ L 365, 1982.

[3] Suspension of imports of all products of Argentine origin (EEC Regulation of 16.4.1982 and decision of the same date by representatives of the Member States of ECSC, OJ L 102, 1982). The stated legal grounds for the regulation were Article 113 of the EEC Treaty.
Cj. P.J. Kuyper, *Community Sanctions against Argentina – Lawfulness under Community and International Law – Essays in European Law and Integration,* K. Kluwer, 1984.

Section 6: Territorial application of Community agreements

Article 29 of the 1969 Vienna Convention on the Law of Treaties simply states that, unless otherwise provided, a treaty concluded between States applies to the entire territory of the States concerned. The question of the territorial application of treaties and agreements to which international organizations are parties was considered by the International Law Commission when it was working on its 'draft articles' (previously mentioned) concerning treaties between States and international organizations or between two or more international organizations. The Commission found that, in most cases, it was inappropriate to speak of the territory of an international organization and that, in any case, the duties, institutional rules and practices of international organizations varied too widely for there to be any possibility of adopting a general provision to cover the territorial application of treaties and agreements which they conclude. The International Law Commission, therefore, decided not to include any specific provision on this subject in its 'draft articles'.

The European Communities, of course, have no territories of their own but the Treaties establishing them contain very precise and highly complicated provisions as to the territories where those Treaties apply and all instruments of 'derived' law adopted by the Community institutions apply to those same territories, unless there is express provision to the contrary.

The same applies to international agreements concluded by the Communities with non-member countries and this is the point which concerns us here.

A – Territory to which the Treaties establishing the Communities apply

The three Treaties – ECSC, EEC and EAEC – do not apply to exactly the same territory. Moreover, the authors of those Treaties gave them very different status because of the special legal, geographical, economic or social features of some of the territories under the sovereignty, jurisdiction or administration of the Member States.

All the provisions of the ECSC, EEC and EAEC Treaties naturally apply to the 'European' territories of the Member States. They apply under certain conditions only to the Channel Islands, the Isle of Man[1] and Gibraltar.[2] They do not apply to the Faeroe

---

[1] Article 227(5) (c) of the EEC Treaty, Article 79(2) (c) of the ECSC Treaty, Article 198(3) (d) of the EAEC Treaty; Protocol No 3 annexed to the instruments of accession to the European Communities of the United Kingdom, Denmark and Ireland.

[2] EEC Treaty, Article 227(4) (European territory 'for whose external relations a Member State is responsible'; ECSC Treaty, Article 79, paragraph 1, second sentence; EAEC Treaty, Article 198, paragraph 2; Article 28 of the instrument of accession to the European Communities of the United Kingdom, Denmark and Ireland).

Islands[1] and ceased to apply as from 1 February 1985 to Greenland[2] although those two territories are an integral part of the Kingdom of Denmark. There is also the special problem of the western sectors of Berlin which will be further considered later (p. 133).

Outside Europe, this situation is even more complicated.

The ECSC Treaty does not apply to any of the non-European territories of Member States.[3] The opposite is true for the EAEC Treaty which applies to all 'non-European territories under the jurisdiction' of Member States.[4]

The EEC Treaty is more selective. Some of its provisions apply in full to the French Overseas Departments. The remainder do not apply there unless the Council of the Communities unanimously decides to the contrary.[5]

The French Overseas Territories, the Dutch West Indies and the overseas countries and territories which 'have special relations' with the United Kingdom and are listed in an annex to the EEC Treaty[6] are not, strictly speaking, included in the territories to which the EEC Treaty applies and international agreements concluded by the EEC with non-member countries do not apply there. These territories are only covered by a system of 'association' laid down by the Council of the Communities, which, since 1975, has closely followed the pattern of the arrangements enjoyed by the independent ACP States under the terms of the Lomé Conventions.[7]

B – The 'territorial clause' in Community international agreements

So that there can be no doubts in the minds of States with which the Communities conclude international agreements, it has become practice to include a clause settling the

---

[1] EEC Treaty, Article 227(5)(a); ECSC Treaty, Article 79(2)(a); EAEC Treaty, Article 198(3)(a); Protocol No 2 annexed to the instrument of accession to the European Communities of the United Kingdom, Denmark and Ireland.

[2] When Denmark acceded to the Communities (1973), Greenland was included in the territory to which the ECSC, EEC and EAEC Treaties applied, subject to the terms of Protocol No 4 annexed to the instrument of accession to the Communities of the United Kingdom, Denmark and Ireland (OJ L 73, 1972). On 23.2.1982, the people of Greenland decided by referendum to leave the Communities and the Danish Government supported their demand. After consulting the Commission (Bulletin EC 1-1983, pp. 13-15) and the European Parliament (OJ 184, 1983), the Council approved, on 20.2.1984, and the Member States signed on 13.3.1984, an agreement on future relations between Greenland and the Community. By virtue of this agreement (OJ L 29, 1985), which has been ratified by the parliaments of all Member States, Greenland ceased to belong to the Community as from 1.2.1985. From then it benefits, with certain reservations, from the arrangements applied to overseas countries and territories associated with the Community (see below). In addition, there are special provisions governing imports of Greenland fisheries products into the Community and fishing by Member States vessels in Greenland waters (see protocols of 13.3.1984, OJ L 29, 1985).

[3] ECSC Treaty, Article 79.

[4] Excluding non-European territories having special relations with the United Kingdom and not listed in Annex IV to the EEC Treaty, Hong Kong in particular (EAEC Treaty, Article 198, para. 1).

[5] EEC Treaty, Article 227(2); Order of the CJ, 10.10.1978, Case 148/77 *Hansen* [1978] ECR 1787.

[6] Annex IV (which excludes Hong Kong in particular).

[7] Association arrangements approved by Decision of the Council of the European Communities of 16.12.1980 (OJ L 361, 1980).

question of territorial application, in the text of agreements and in particular of bilateral agreements.

The clause is worded as follows: 'This agreement applies to the territories to which the Treaty establishing the European Economic Community applies, on the terms and conditions laid down in that Treaty.'

In our opinion two questions concerning the territory to which international agreements concluded by the European Communities apply call for special consideration.

The first is the extension of such agreements to the western sectors of Berlin.

The second is how States which have concluded international agreements with the Communities are affected by the subsequent accession of new Member States to the Communities.

1. Extension of Community international agreements to the western sectors of Berlin[1]

The inclusion in Community bilateral agreements of the territorial clause reproduced above normally gives rise to no difficulties with the States which negotiate such agreements, as the exact significance and scope of that clause are explained to them while negotiations are in progress and it now appears in virtually all bilateral agreements concluded by the Communities.

On the other hand, difficulties have always arisen over acceptance of the territorial clause when the Communities have negotiated bilateral agreements with East European countries. The difficulty lies in the extension of such agreements to the western sectors of Berlin.

It is a fact that neither the Soviet Union nor the three allied powers (France, United Kingdom and United States) consider the western sectors of Berlin to be part of the territory of the Federal Republic of Germany (FRG).[2] The three allied powers agreed, however, that the laws, regulations and international agreements of the Federal Republic of Germany could apply, under their control, to the western sectors of Berlin.[3]

When the Treaties establishing the European Communities were signed, the government of the Federal Republic of Germany reserved the right to declare that those Trea-

---

[1] See in particular: W. Wengler, *'Berlin-Ouest et les Communautés européennes'*, Annuaire français de droit international, 1978, p. 217 et seq.; R. de Rosa, *'Lo status internazionale de Berlino-Ovest e i suoi reflessi nella Comunità economica europea'*, La Comunità internazionale, Padua, Vol. XX6, 1981, p. 395 et seq.

[2] See quadripartite agreement (United States, USSR, United Kingdom, France) of 3.9.1971, part II. Provisions concerning the western sectors of Berlin, B. 'The Governments of the French Republic, of the United Kingdom of Great Britain and Northern Ireland and of the United States of America declare that the links between the western sectors of Berlin and the Federal Republic of Germany shall be maintained and developed, taking due account of the fact that those sectors continue not to form part of the Federal Republic of Germany and not to be governed by it'.

[3] See textual references in W. Wengler, op. cit.

ties would apply also to the western sectors of Berlin.[1] This declaration was made and was approved by the three allied powers. They also agreed that 'derived' Community law and international agreements concluded by the Communities with non-member countries should apply to West Berlin.

For a long time, the USSR opposed the extension to West Berlin of the laws, regulations and international agreements of the Federal Republic of Germany.
This opposition was withdrawn when the quadripartite agreement on Berlin was signed in 1971.[2]

On the other hand, the USSR has continued to oppose any extension to the western sectors of Berlin of original and 'derived' Community law and of Community international agreements.

Hence the difficulties experienced by the Communities in gaining acceptance for the inclusion in bilateral agreements negotiated with East European countries of the territorial clause quoted above, in which the words 'and on the terms and conditions laid down in that Treaty' apply to the western sectors of Berlin.

Among the negotiations which failed on this issue were those for the fisheries agreement between the EEC and the USSR. The same question was also one of the reasons for the failure of the negotiations started by the EEC with the Council for Mutual Economic Assistance (Comecon) with a view to the normalization of relations between the EEC and the member countries of that organization.

By contrast, it has not prevented the conclusion of some commercial arrangements or agreements with East European countries: 1980 EEC-Romania agreement (previously mentioned) on trade in industrial products, agreements on trade in textiles between the EEC and Bulgaria and the EEC and Poland.[3] These agreements include the territorial clause which applies, in particular to the western sectors of Berlin, but, when these agreements were signed, the East European countries involved made unilateral declara-

---

[1] Declaration made when the EEC and EAEC Treaties were signed in Rome on 25.3.1957. The same declaration was made by the Federal Republic of Germany:
  (i) when the Treaty establishing a single Council and Commission for the European Communities was signed in Brussels on 8.4.1965 (OJ 152, 1967) (application of this Treaty and the ECSC Treaty to Berlin);
  (ii) when the Treaty concerning the accession to the European Communities of the United Kingdom, Denmark and Ireland was signed in Brussels on 22.1.1972 (OJ L 73, 1972);
  (iii) when the Treaty concerning the accession to the European Communities of the Hellenic Republic was signed in Athens on 28.5.1979 (OJ L 291, 1979).
[2] Quadripartite agreement (previously mentioned), Annex IV-B, declaration by the Government of the USSR: '2. Provided questions of security and status are not affected, (the Government of the USSR) will not raise any objection to ... (b) in accordance with the established procedure, the extension to the western sectors of Berlin of international agreements and arrangements concluded by the Federal Republic of Germany, provided that the extension of such agreements and arrangements is specifically stipulated in each case.'
[3] These agreements are among the 26 bilateral agreements mentioned on p. 65 (note 1).

tions to the effect that the said agreements in no way affected the status of Berlin as established by the quadripartite agreement of 1971.

It was only on that condition that the countries concerned agreed to the inclusion of the Berlin clause in agreements linking them with the Communities.

The importance of this clause is chiefly political, but it also has legal and practical aspects. It is, in fact, essential in order to allow persons and firms established in the western sectors of Berlin, and the goods and services which they can export to non-member countries,[1] to benefit from international agreements concluded by the Communities.

2. Effects of the subsequent accession of new Member States on States which have previously concluded international agreements with the European Communities

(a) Principle of the extension of agreements to the new Member States

Subject to the essential transitional measures, the 'new' Member States of the Communities (United Kingdom, Ireland and Denmark, as from 1 January 1973; Greece, as from 1 January 1981) agreed to be bound, as from their accession, by the ECSC, EEC and EAEC Treaties and by all instruments, declarations resolutions and other provisions previously adopted by the Community institutions.

The treaties of accession[2] also stipulated that the States concerned would be bound by 'Community' international agreemeents previously concluded by any of the Communities with one or more non-member countries. By virtue of the same Treaties,[3] the new Member States undertook to accede to agreements concluded jointly by any of the Communities and the 'original' Member States ('mixed' agreements), and to 'connected' agreements concluded by those States, that is agreements concluded by the Member States of the ECSC, supplementing commercial or association agreements concluded by the EEC.[4]

The instruments of accession listed – limitatively – the bilateral agrreements ('Community' and 'mixed') which the new Member States were required to apply as from

---

[1] Thus, firms established in Berlin are entitled, like those established in the Member States of the Communities, to tender for contracts financed with the aid of funds provided by the EEC under its policy for aid to developing countries (ACP States, parties to the Lomé Convention; overseas countries and territories associated with the EEC; Mediterranean countries linked to the EEC by agreements including provision for financial aid; 'non-associated' developing countries).

[2] Article 4, paragraph 1, of the instrument of accession to the European Communities of the United Kingdom, Denmark and Ireland, annexed to the Treaty of Brussels of 22.1.1972; Article 4, paragraph 1 of the instrument of accession to the European Communities of the Hellenic Republic, annexed to the Treaty of Athens of 28.5.1979.

[3] Article 4, paragraph 2, of each of the 'instruments of accession' referred to in note 2 above.

[4] On these agreements, see Part Two above, p. 67, note 4.

their accession.[1] They also specified[2] that any transitional measures or adaptations which might prove necessary would be specified in individual protocols with the non-member contracting countries.

The authors of the Treaty and instrument of accession of the United Kingdom, Denmark and Ireland laid down no precise timetable for the negotiation of these protocols. Nor were any provisions agreed between the Community and the States wishing to accede, regarding the position to be taken by the Communities in these negotiations.

As the applicant States did not press the Communities to conclude amending protocols with certain non-member countries, which themselves showed little interest in making a move, some protocols were not concluded and brought into force until after 1 January 1973 or even failed to appear; and for varying lengths of time after their accession the new Member States did not apply or applied partially only the agreements whose adaptation had given rise to the difficulties.

In the light of this experience, when the accession of Greece was being negotiated, the Community representatives agreed in exact terms with the Greek representatives the adaptations which would have to be made to the international agreements which the new Member State would have to apply,[3] and started talks with the non-member countries concerned very early, so that the amending protocols could, where possible, be concluded with them before the effective entry of Greece into the Common Market. Anticipating likely delays on these discussions, the authors of the treaty and instrument of accession for Greece, stipulated that if, for reasons beyond the control of the Community or of Greece, the amending protocols were not concluded before 1 January 1981, the Community would take the necessary measures (independently) to correct the situation as from the date of accession.[4]

(b) Automatic extension or renegotiation?

During negotiation of the amending protocols, some of the non-member countries involved had differing interests and took totally opposed positions as regards the need for and scope of negotiations.

---

[1] Instrument of accession of the United Kingdom, Denmark and Ireland, Article 108(3): agreements with Turkey, Tunisia, Morocco, Israel, Spain and Malta; instrument of accession of Greece, Articles 120, 122 and 123: agreements with Algeria, Austria, Cyprus, Spain, Egypt, Finland, Iceland, Israel, Jordan, Lebanon, Malta, Morocco, Norway, Portugal, Sweden, Switzerland, Syria, Tunisia and Turkey; Lomé II Convention, 1979; Multifibre Arrangements of 1973 and bilateral arrangements concluded by the EEC under that multilateral arrangement.

[2] Instrument of accession of the United Kingdom, Denmark and Ireland, Article 108(1); instrument of accession of Greece, Articles 118 and 123.

[3] See joint declaration annexed to the Greek instrument of accession, concerning protocols to be concluded with certain non-member countries in accordance with Article 118, 'For the negotiation of the protocols to be concluded with the non-member contracting countries referred to in Article 118, the Community will negotiate on the basis of the relevant terms agreed at the conference between the European Communities and the Hellenic Republic'.

[4] Instrument of accession of Greece, Articles 119 and 123(2).

Austria and other Member States of the European Free Trade Association argued, for example, that the ('Community') trade agreements which they had concluded with the EEC in 1972-73 should apply automatically to Greece and that the 'concessions' which they enjoyed on the market of the original Member States as a result of these agreements should also be allowed them on the Greek market, subject solely to the same transitional provisions as any stipulated for the progressive removal of the remaining barriers to trade in the same products between the EEC and the new Member State.

Conversely, certain States linked to the EEC by way of a 'joint' cooperation agreement argued that the accession of Greece to the Communities did not require them to apply that agreement to the new Member State. In any event, they argued that the extension of the agreement to Greece would alter the balance of the concessions previously agreed and that it was necessary therefore to renegotiate those concessions and not simply to adapt the agreement. This was the position of the Maghreb countries in particular.

The negotiating positions adopted by some of the Communities' partners prevented the conclusion of all the protocols before 1 January 1981 and the Council of the Communities had to act independently to adopt transitional measures governing relations between Greece and the countries concerned;[1] these measures were in fact less favourable than those the Communities had been prepared to grant in a negotiated protocol. All the amending protocols required by the accession of Greece were finally signed and put into force. As was to be expected, the arrangements did not wholly satisfy either the supporters of straightforward automatic extension or the advocates of complete renegotiation.

(c) Distinction between 'Community' and 'mixed' agreements

The question as to how States which have concluded international agreements with the European Communities are affected by the subsequent addition of one or more new Member States to the Communities appears to call for quite different answers according to whether the agreements are 'Community' agreements, like those linking the EEC with the EFTA countries or 'mixed' agreements, like those linking the EEC to the Maghreb and Mashreq countries and to the ACP countries (Lomé Convention), even though both contain the 'territorial clause' quoted earlier.

It will be recalled that this clause refers to 'territories where the Treaty establishing the EEC applies' without specifying whether this relates solely to territories to which the said Treaty applies at present or whether it can also cover territories where the same Treaty will also apply, following the accession of a new State to the Community. It would seem unlikely that any State which negotiates and concludes an agreement with any one of the Communities can be unaware that the Communities are liable to be enlarged to take in new European countries or that the clause referred to earlier can cover

---

[1] See for example (OJ L 373, 1981 and 190, 1982) the measures adopted by the Council of the European Communities for the transitional regulation (until 31.12.1982) of relations between Greece and the ACP States, parties to the Lomé II Convention.

such cases. At least such a State should have the meaning and scope of that clause explained to it by Community negotiators.

This being so, it would seem reasonable to accept the principle of the argument that 'Community' agreements concluded by non-member countries with the Communities before their enlargement should be extended automatically to the new Member States.[1]

In the case of 'mixed' agreements, this thesis cannot easily be sustained, however, because the consent of one State to be linked with other named States cannot create obligations for that first State, nor even vest rights in it in relation to a third State.[2] Furthermore, 'mixed' agreements fall far short in some cases of identifying exactly the matters for which the Community and the signatory Member States respectively have jurisdiction. That being so, the inclusion of the 'territorial clause' in such agreements would not appear to be capable of ensuring automatic extension to new Member States. Extension is possible only by renegotiation of the agreement.

It may be asked whether this strongly affirmative proposition might not be toned down in the particular case of the provisions relating to trade included in the association or cooperation agreements concluded by the EEC and its Member States and frequently applied by the EEC alone, by virtue of an interim agreement concluded with the non-member country or countries concerned, without waiting until completion of the ratification procedures allows the whole agreement to enter into force between the parties.[3]

Cannot such provisions, clearly identified as within the competence of the EEC, be treated as a 'Community' agreement, automatically extended to new Member States if the Communities are enlarged? We do not believe so, because this would overlook the fact that the parties regard the provisions of an agreement and particularly of a 'mixed' agreement as forming an indivisible whole. Furthermore, the thesis that the 'Community' parts of a 'mixed' agreement are governed by the principle of automatic extension would have little practical effect because the rest of the agreement would have to be renegotiated in any case.

Our final view is that no sharp distinction can be made between 'Community' and 'mixed' agreements, as regards their possible extension to new Member States.

Once an agreement of either category has been negotiated with a country in the political and economic context of a Community with N members, it is idle to suppose that it can be applied to a Community with N + 1, 2 or 3 members without any change of substance. Experience has shown that adaptations have always been necessary and that,

---

[1] Provided, of course, these agreements include the territorial clause mentioned previously on p. 133. It may be noted that as an exception to the normal practice, the 1982 arrangement whereby the ECSC undertook to limit its exports of certain iron and steel products to the United States between 1.11.1982 and 31.12.1985 (see Part Two above p. 66), applies only to the territories to which the Treaty establishing the ECSC 'as presently constituted applies on the conditions laid down in that Treaty'.

[2] See Articles 35 and 36 of the 1969 Vienna Convention on the Law of Treaties.

[3] See for example the interim EEC-Yugoslavia agreement of 6.5.1980 (OJ L 130, 1980).

once that is so, the negotiations which have to be opened with the non-member country concerned cannot be kept within limits strictly defined in advance by either of the parties. The negotiation of the amending protocols made necessary by Greece's accession merely proved that the automatic element resulting from the 'territorial clause' could, where appropriate, provide the Community or its partners with a valid argument against challenging the bases of the agreement.

Chapter II – The Communities and international liability

Any subject of international law who causes damage to another subject may be called upon to answer for it and to make reparation.

This liability, limited exclusively to the field of international law is generally based on the concept of an unlawful international act. International law does not yet recognize 'unoffending' liability except under the terms of special agreements (Convention of 29 March 1972 on liability for damage caused by space objects).

An unlawful act originates from any breach of an international commitment, including any breach of obligations arising from treaties or customary rules.

International case-law is a fundamental element in international law.[1] It must be added, however, that there have been relatively few cases of a State being sued in exclusively legal terms and by an exclusively legal procedure. The most frequent case rulings – chiefly by arbitration – have been decisions given when diplomatic privilege has been claimed in respect of damage caused by a State to the person or property of foreign nationals. This is the reason why the first attempts at codification – which have not succeeded – have been directed to this aspect of international liability.[2]

It was not until 1973 that the International Law Commission first turned its attention to codification of the rules concerning liability of States and this major task has not yet been completed.

It must also be realized that international society is little subject to any jurisdiction, with the result that liability is more a reference than a current element in practice.

With the growth of international organizations and their activities, the question was bound to arise of whether such subjects can be involved in issues of liability.

---

[1] 'It is a principle of international law and even a general legal concept that any breach of an undertaking involves the obligation to make reparation' (judgment of the International Court of Justice in the case of the Chorzow factory, A/17, p. p. 25-29).

[2] 1930 conference under the auspices of the League of Nations; work subsequently taken up by the International Law Commission but abandoned because views were too divergent. As regards the current work of the ILC, see in particular, *ILC Yearbook,* 1975, Vol. II, pp.60-64 and the Commission's reports to the General Assembly since 1975.

Practice – which is very limited — and doctrine (with a few exceptions) both indicate that this is the case. As holders of rights in the international order, organizations also have obligations. Liability is the corollary to failure to fulfil an obligation.

A few cases confirm both that an international organization can sue a State[1] and can equally be sued for unlawful acts committed by its organs or agents.[2]

Similarly, in a very special case such as that of damage caused by space objects, the treaty of 29 March 1972 could not – despite the reluctance of some States – exclude the possibility that the launching organizations might be liable.

Lastly, the procedures – in particular arbitration – for the settlement of disputes involving organizations are implicitly based on the fact that an organization can be found guilty of an unlawful act attributable to it.

In the case of the Communities, the first reaction here might be to consider that the rules of the liability apply to them as to any other international organization and that no specific theory is required for them.

We believe this to be correct. There is in fact no reason to consider that the Communities should be accorded special treatment in the matter. In other words, the presumption is that all the rules of customary international law apply to the Communities.

Nevertheless, the Communities could be a source of particular difficulties because of their special structure, the sharing of powers with the Member States and the use of 'mixed agreements'.

The difficulties can only be discussed as a future possibility because there has as yet been no actual case where the Communities have been charged with either passive or active international liability.[3]

Section 1: 'Passive' liability of the Communities

If the Communities were sued by another subject of international law, the only difficulty would be to decide whether the Community or the Member States were responsible for the unlawful act.

Several possible cases have to be considered.

---

[1] Case of damage suffered in the service of the United Nations, International Court of Justice, Opinion, *Reports,* 1949, p.184.

[2] Opinion of the International Court of Justice of 20.7.1962. Compensation payable by the United Nations for damage caused by the peace-keeping forces in the Congo, *Reports,* ICJ, 1962, p.150. See P. de Visscher, '*Observations sur le fondement et la mise en oeuvre du principe de la responsabilite de l'ONU*', Annales de droit et de science politique, Vol. 23, No 3.

[3] Leaving aside as a matter of purely internal law, the question of how jurisdiction would be shared between the Commission and the Council, in taking the necessary decisions in a case involving liability.

A – *Liability without reference to the implementation of an agreement*

By hypothesis, failure to comply with the general rules of international law constitutes liability.

Any charge presumes that the plaintiff must establish liability. He has to show that the alleged unlawful act was committed by the person he accuses.

It may be difficult to establish the facts and the action may be misdirected. If a plaintiff sues a Member State when he should have sued the Community, his action will fail, but this would not prevent him from proceeding again on different grounds.

Should it be argued that because of the specific character of the Community and the complexity of the division of powers between itself and the Member States, the rules governing answerability should be relaxed so that a plaintiff could for example sue both the Community and the Member State of liability at the same time?

This is not our view.

International practice already covers cases of the complex division of powers where this has not prevented strict application of the rules governing answerability in court rulings.[1]

The decision on the issue of answerability assumes that the plaintiff briefs himself on the division of powers between the Community and the Member States by the means at his disposal.

This is a perfectly normal procedure. It is difficult to see how a plaintiff could claim to be unaware of the division.[2]

The only real question relates to the criteria to be applied in determining whether the Community or a Member State is liable in a complicated case.

The problem of State or Community liability might arise, for example, in the case of damage caused by a State official acting to implement a Community regulation.[3]

---

[1] See for example, the *Chevreau* case, 9.6.1931, *Records of arbitration judgments,* Vol. II, p.1113 (exercise of consular functions by one State on behalf of another).

[2] Thus in the case of damage caused to the diplomatic mission to the Community of a n-member State, the liability of the State where the headquarters are located has to be established, because nder the terms of the Protocol on Privileges and Immunities it is that State which is responsible for ensuring iat such missions receive the treatment to which they are entitled.
It is quite normal that the plaintiff State should be aware of the position and should address its protest to the State where the headquarters are located and not to the Community.

[3] Problems already referred to the Court of Justice in connection with Community law, see judgment of 14.7.1967, Joined Cases 5, 7 and 13 to 24/66 *Kampffmeyer* [1967] ECR 332; judgment of 13.2.1979, Case 101/78 *Granaria* [1979] ECR 623.

In our view, the Community is liable unless the plaintiff can prove that the State official has committed an offence 'separate' from the strict implementation of the regulation in question. This interpretation is, moreover, in conformity with the rule formulated by the International Law Commission for strictly inter-State relations. Under the draft articles formulated by the Commission, an unlawful act commited by a State acting under the control and direction of another State renders the second State liable.

There are other possible cases to which only practice can supply the answer.

At this stage, the important point, in our view, is that the defendant – whether the Community or a Member State – must contest the admissibility of the action if it considers it to be misdirected.[1] Failure to do so, in the expectation of a subsequent 'action' against the subject really liable, would inevitably create confusion for third parties.

B – Liability with reference to the implementation of an agreement

There are two possible cases: first that of a 'Community' agreement and secondly that of a 'mixed' agreement.

1. Community agreement

In accordance with the general rules applying the contracts and treaties, one party to a treaty can be sued only by another party.

Consequently, if an agreement is not properly implemented, the other party or parties should bring their action against the Community.

Here again, however, account must be taken of the terms of Article 228, paragraph 2, which provides that Member States are bound by Community agreements.

If need be, this provision confirms that the Community could not claim default on the part of one or more Member States[2] as grounds for non-fulfilment of an agreement.

It also entitles the other contracting party to bring an action against the Community on the grounds that one or more Member States have not implemented the agreement properly, as those States are agents for the implementation of the Community agreement.[3]

---

[1] This should apply particularly in the case of an action brought by a State 'not recognizing' the Communities and, therefore, addressing itself systematically to the Member States.

[2] An agreement like the Fisheries Agreement of 15.2.1977 between the Community and the United States lays particular stress on the liability of the Community by requiring it to take all necessary measures to ensure that the nationals and vessels of Member States comply with the provisions of the agreement.

[3] The Community could then proceed against the 'defaulting' Member State through the Community system and its processes.

There is also the possibility of the opposite case where the other contracting party proceeds against the Member States because it cannot obtain the measures to which it believes itself to be entitled from the Communities themselves.

Such an action would appear to disregard the relative effect of treaties because it would be brought against subjects not parties to the agreement. Furthermore, it would weaken the concept of Communities independent of their Member States.

It is nevertheless the logical conclusion of the reasoning outlined by the Court in the *Kupferberg* case, to the effect that 'by ensuring fulfilment of the undertakings arising from an agreement concluded by the Community institutions, Member States fulfil an obligation to the non-member countries concerned'.

On this view, Article 228(2) constitutes a stipulation for others which third parties can invoke in their case. Having failed in an action against the Community, the other contracting party would be entitled to use this article, in addition to the terms of the Community agreement, as grounds for an action against the Member States.[1]

However, this situation is very unlikely to arise because it is not easy to see what advantage the Community could gain by hiding behind its Member States in such a manner.

2. 'Mixed' agreement

By virtue of the principles of contract law, the other contracting party could *a priori* proceed against both the Community and the Member States. The question is therefore against which of them he should proceed.

In our view, the answer depends on the terms of the agreement.

In the case of an agreement which clearly specifies the matters for which the Community and its Member States are respectively answerable, and, even more so, if it is accompanied by a list of obligations, as in the case of the Convention on the Law of the Sea, the plaintiff should proceed against the Community or one or more of its Member States, as appropriate.[2]

---

[1] In its comments to the Secretary-General of the United Nations on the draft articles formulated by the ILC concerning treaties concluded between States and international organizations, the EEC stated, with particular reference to Article 228(2) 'It might even be said that this provision of the EEC Treaty can be regarded as a treaty provision designed to offer guarantees for non-member States, which the States concerned accept when concluding a treaty with the organization' (doc. A/36/10, p.496).

[2] By what we regard as excessive caution, Article 6 of Annex IX to the Convention on the Law of the Sea stipulates that 'any State party to the Convention may require an international organization or its member States parties to the Convention to specify which of them is liable in a particular case. The organization and member States concerned must provide this information. If they fail to do so within a reasonable time or if they supply contradictory information, they will be held jointly and severally liable'. This provision creates a privileged position for the other contracting parties because they should, in normal circumstances, have to establish answerability in each individual case by reference to the list of obligations notified to them. The special arrangements instituted by this convention, of course, take precedence over the general rules.

If, on the other hand, the division of obligations between the Community and the Member States is not clear, it would be difficult to maintain that the plaintiff cannot proceed against both the Community and the Member States, claiming that they are jointly liable. One or other could then decide to assume liability towards the contracting party.[1]

Section 2: 'Active' Community liability

The Communities can proceed against a subject of international law for damage caused to them by action or omission.

In addition, on the basis of the theory of protection by function, established by the International Court of Justice in the *Count Bernadotte* case, they might demand compensation from a third party for damages caused to one of their officials.[2]

In both cases, the general rules of international liability apply to the Communities without any specific features being involved.[3]

On the other hand, there is the much more delicate question of whether the Communities could sue a third party for damage suffered by a national of a Member State. It is of course usual for States to take such action on grounds of 'diplomatic protection'. It is also a fact that diplomatic protection is governed by strict rules, in particular that of 'nationality'.

Under this rule, any claim based on diplomatic protection for a private individual is admissible only if the person concerned holds the nationality of the plaintiff. The only exception to that rule is precisely that furnished by the theory of protection by function which, as already noted, can apply only to personal damage suffered by 'officials'.

As things stand at present, there is no 'Community nationality'.

Cases could arise, however, where it might be necessary for the Communities to start an action of that kind.

---

[1] The provisions of Article 228(2) apply *mutatis mutandis* to the 'Community parts' of a 'mixed' agreement. In its aforementioned comments on the draft articles of the ILC, the EEC stated: 'The Community considers that it should be clear that in the case of joint agreements Articles 36 bis (of the draft) applies also to the rights and obligations embodied in the agreement which are within the jurisdiction of the international organization (ibid. p.497).

[2] See the previously–mentioned opinion of the International Court of Justice concerning compensation for certain damages suffered in the service of the United Nations. The term 'official' has to be widely interpreted as applying to any person suffering damage while acting on behalf of the organization.

[3] The Communities might have to claim against a State which does not recognize them. This involves a further difficulty in applying the rules of liability but a State could find itself in the same situation.

Thus, taking the example of the fisheries agreement concluded by the EEC with a non-member State, it could happen that a fisherman from a Member State suffered damage through the failure of the State contracting with the Community to implement the provisions of the agreement.

In such a case, the State of which the fisherman was a national could bring an action against the non-member country by virtue of the normal rules of diplomatic protection. But, not being a party to the fisheries agreement, the principle of the related effect of treaties could be used against the State concerned and it might not be able to claim non-implementation of the agreement.

Even supposing that the defendant allowed the plaintiff State to invoke the clauses of the agreement to which it was not party,[1] the situation could not be regarded as legally satisfactory because it would hide the Communities, which have sole responsibility for the common fisheries policy, behind the Member States.

In this situation, therefore, the Communities demand based on damage suffered by a private individual should logically be admitted.

This would require an extension of the right to diplomatic protection. The same result could be achieved either by an extension of the concept of nationality or by a new use of the concept of protection by function.

Undoubtedly, diplomatic protection has to be taken into consideration, principally from the standpoint of its purpose. The strict application of the traditional rules would inevitably make it into a petrified institution out of touch with modern requirements.

---

[1] In this case again, Article 228(2) of the EEC Treaty might be invoked on the grounds that by creating obligations towards the Member States it also implicitly creates rights for them.

Chapter III – The Communities and the peaceful settlement of disputes

The various settlement procedures have clearly followed the pattern of State practice.

The methods of settlement are either 'optional' or 'compulsory'. The first type of settlement is agreed spontaneously by the parties without reference to any pre-established obligation. The second is based on a clause included beforehand in a bilateral or multilateral treaty, under the terms of which, in the event of a dispute within the limits of the treaty, the parties are 'required' in principle to have recourse to the settlement procedures laid down. The effectiveness of this obligation depends greatly on the way the settlement clause is drafted and, in particular, on the ways of overcoming a refusal by one party to apply the set procedure.

From the standpoint of the effects of the procedure, a distinction has to be made between a settlement of optional effect and a settlement of compulsory effect. The first category includes all cases where the procedure can only result in proposals to the parties. This covers conciliation, mediation and the adoption of recommendations by an international body. The second category includes a decision by a court or a decision by the institution of an organization, when it has powers to decide the issue.

It is probably necessary to add a third category which modern practice is tending to develop, namely what might be called 'institutionalized negotiation' within the managing body for an international agreement (joint committee, etc.).

Generally speaking, States are fairly willing to include dispute settlement clauses in their agreements, but become distrustful and restrictive when such clauses involve a settlement which is compulsory without an escape clause.

That is why actual reference to arbitration and to the International Court of Justice remains the exception in practice.

This is even more true in the case of States which refuse these methods of settlement on principle. This applies to the Soviet Union, the East European States and more widely all the Marxist States.

In the final analysis, the basic instrument for the settlement of disputes is still as it always has been, negotiation, which does not necessarily lead to a settlement but often to a deadlock.

If the dispute does not involve the parties' vital interests, this situation can continue without much damage to the international community.

One further general point should be emphasized: the peaceful settlement of disputes depends essentially on a willingness to settle. The parties can modify the procedures without limit according to their needs and circumstances.

Although the principle of peaceful settlement is of greater importance for States because of the extremes to which their disputes can be carried, there is no reason why international organizations, which are playing an increasingly active part in international life, should not be allowed to use the procedures for the settlement of disputes.

Their position in this respect can be summarized as follows:

(a) By virtue of their legal immunity, which can now be regarded as established by custom, international organizations are not normally answerable to domestic courts.[1] Their disputes with a Member State or a non-member State are a matter of international law and subject to international settlement procedures.

(b) Under the terms of the Statute of the International Court of Justice (Article 36), international organizations cannot be parties to a dispute referred to that court, which is open to States only. Because this is so, a number of substitutes have been found, such as the provisions whereby, in the event of a dispute with a State, an organization can – if so authorized – ask the court for a consultative opinion, which will be regarded as binding on the parties to the dispute (agreement on headquarters between the UN and the United States, of 31 October 1947, Article 21).

(c) Apart from this particular restriction, international organizations can make use of all known techniques for the settlement of disputes both with each other and with States. They in fact use those techniques in the agreements which they conclude with each other and with States. Arbitration clauses, in particular, are fairly common, because, as already stated, organizations have no access to the International Court of Justice.

(d) Practice is very limited at present as regards not the settlement clauses but the settlement procedures actually followed by organizations.

It cannot be claimed, therefore, that a set of principles to which reference can be made has already been formulated.

Community practice is non-existent as regards the actual use of a procedure for the peaceful settlement of disputes outside the scope of diplomatic negotiations.

Reference cannot be made, therefore, to the dispute settlement clauses which have been included in agreements to which the Community is a party or may become a party.

As was to be expected, this examination reveals a very wide variety of procedures.

---

[1] The principle was stated in a decision handed down by the Italian Supreme Court of Appeal on 26.2.1931 in the *Profili* case.
See J. Duffar, *Contribution a l'étude des privilèges et immunités des organisations internationales,* Librairie générale de droit et de jurisprudence, Paris, 1982, in particular p.59 *et seq.*

These need to be described before considering the special problems which they can pose.

Section 1: Settlement procedures laid down in Community agreements

A – *Freedom for the parties and 'institutionalized negotiations'*

Some agreements simply state the principle of settlement without specifying any procedure.[1]

The trade agreements concluded with the member States of EFTA set up joint committees to administer the agreement. These committees therefore have to decide on any difficulties which may arise in connection with the implementation of the agreement. There is no settlement procedure if the committees fail to resolve the problem.

B – *Settlement by a body administering the agreement*

All the commodity agreements[2] specify a procedure based on the same principles:
(i) any dispute regarding the interpretation or implementation of the agreement, which is not resolved by negotiation, is referred to the Council for decision, at the request of any member party to the agreement;
(ii) the Council rules on the dispute by a vote taken in accordance with its rules of procedure;
(iii) when a dispute is referred to the Council, a majority or a qualified minority of members may request the Council to take the opinion of an advisory commission set up for the purpose. When this opinion has been given, the Council regains its full powers of decision.[2]

C – *Settlement by arbitration*

An arbitration clause is fairly often included in Community agreements.

---

[1] Previously-mentioned Convention on long-distance transboundary air pollution, Article 13: 'If a dispute arises between two or more contracting parties to this convention, the said parties will seek a solution by negotiation or by any other method of settling disputes which is acceptable to them.'

[2] Coffee, tin, cocoa and other agreements.
Similarly, as the EEC has become a 'member' of the Council of GATT by virtue of its 'succession' to the Member States, it can use the specific settlement procedures of that agreement, which can also be used against the Community.
Thus, on 20.4.1983, the Commission appealed to the Council of GATT against Japan under the terms of Article XXIII(2) of the agreement. This appeal was the second stage of a procedure approved by the Council of the Communities in December 1982.

The procedure follows normal practice: a dispute can only be referred to arbitration after the failure of a first attempt to settle by direct negotiation or negotiation in a body administering the agreement; cases are referred for settlement to an arbitration panel of three members, the first two of whom are appointed by the parties and the third by agreement between the two arbitrators already appointed. If it proves impossible to appoint a third arbitrator, there is usually provision for reference to an outside authority.[1]

D – Settlement by a permanent tribunal

The only example of a Community agreement providing for settlement by a permanent tribunal[2] was the agreement on the establishment of a European Capital Fund for inland navigation.

This agreement, signed on 9 July 1976 by the EEC, the six Member States and Switzerland made provision for a Fund Tribunal to deal with all disputes relating to the interpretation and implementation of the agreement.

There were various procedures for referring cases to this tribunal: appeal for annulment of decisions of Fund authorities, action on grounds of default by those authorities, action on grounds of non-implementation by States.

The tribunal was also empowered to give a preliminary ruling on the interpretation of the agreement by the courts of Member States.

The tribunal was composed of seven judges, one appointed by Switzerland and the other six from the Court of justice of the European Communities.

The settlement procedure established by this agreement was, therefore, highly developed and differed in fairly marked degree from the procedures established within the Community.

At the moment, however, it exists only on paper. When the agreement was referred to the Court of Justice of the European Communites under the terms of Article 228(1) of

---

[1] See for example:

Lomé Convention of 31.10.1979, Article 176.

Fisheries agreement betwen the EEC and Sweden, of 21.3.1977, Article 7 and special annex.

Customs Convention on the international transport of goods under cover of TIR carnets, of 14.11.1975, Article 57.

Convention for the protection of the Rhine against chemical pollution of 1.4.1976, Article 15 and Annex B.

Convention on the protection of the Mediterranean against pollution, of 16.2.1976, Article 22 and Annex A.

Convention for the prevention of marine pollution from land-based sources, Article 21 and Annex B.

It should be noted that when Socialist States are parties to such conventions, they reserve their position on arbitration (for example, the accession of Bulgaria, on 7.11.1977, to the TIR Convention.

[2] Excluding the Convention on the Law of the Sea (1982) to which the EEC can be a party and, like all other parties, could, under the terms of Article 287(a) and Annex IX, Article 7.1, refer a dispute to the International Law of the Sea Tribunal, provided for in Annex VI to the convention.

the EEC Treaty, the Court ruled that it was incompatible with that Treaty.[1] Its entry into force is still pending, therefore.

E – Settlement under a specific procedure laid down in a multilateral general agreement

If the draft articles formulated by the International Law Commission concerning treaties concluded between international organizations and treaties between a State and an organization are approved by a convention, and if the Community is party thereto, the Community will be subject to the provisions regarding the peaceful settlement of disputes. These provisions, transposed from the Vienna Convention on the Law of Treaties stipulate that, if all other procedures fail, any party to a dispute concerning the implementation or interpretation of any article relating to the nullity, extinction or suspension of a treaty, may initiate the procedure laid down in the annex, by addressing a request to the Secretary-General of the United Nations.

This procedure calls for conciliation by a commission appointed in accordance with set rules. The commission's report 'is simply a statement of the recommendations submitted to the parties for consideration to help towards an agreed settlement of the dispute'.

It should also be noted that if the EEC becomes party to the Convention on the Law of the Sea (1982), it will be subject to the terms of Article 7 of Annex IX, which provides that an international organization is free to choose, by written declaration, one or several of the procedures laid down in Article 287, paragraph 1, clauses (a), (c) and (d) for the settlement of disputes.

Part XV of the convention, which deals with the settlement of disputes in fact applies, *mutatis mutandis,* to any dispute between the parties to the convention, one or more of which are international organizations.

F – Settlement by a Community institution

This procedure is confined to the association agreement with Turkey.[2]

This agreement provides that the Association Council may decide to settle disputes or may refer them to the Court of Justice of the European Communites or any other existing judicial body.

There is, however, provision for arbitration if the Association Council fails to reach a decision on the dispute.[3]

---

[1] Opinion 1/76 of 26.4.1977, [1977] ECR 747 to 765.
[2] The same procedure was laid down in the former agreement associating Greece with the EEC (1961).
[3] Association Agreement with Turkey of 12.9.1963, Article 25.

The possibility of reference to the Court of Justice for a settlement has been criticized, because it could be claimed that, as a Community institution, the Court might be both judge and party in the case.

It should be added, however, that a dispute can only be referred to the Court by the Association Council, that is by agreement between the two parties. The Community's contracting partner could not, therefore, be taken to the Court against its wishes.

Section 2: Problems raised by the application to the Communities of procedures for the peaceful settlement of disputes

The foregoing review of the situation might give the impression that the Communities have no objections and foresee no difficulties, if provisions for the settlement of disputes are included in agreements. The truth is somewhat different.

There have in fact been a number of warnings concerning participation by the Communities in arbitration or procedures involving a decision by a tribunal.

The decision reached by the Court of Justice in Opinion 1/76 itself reflects these doubts concerning the involvement of such bodies.

A – Intervention by an outside body into the province of Community law creates the risk of an interpretation conflicting with that of the Court of Justice of the European Communities

In Opinion 1/76, the Court of Justice deemed it appropriate to recall with reference to the 'Fund tribunal' that an agreement concluded by the Community was an 'instrument adopted by one of the institutions' 'with the consequence that the Court is competent, within the Community legal system, to give a preliminary ruling on the interpretation of such an agreement'.

The Court went on to say: 'This raises the question whether the provisions relating to the jurisdiction of the Fund tribunal are compatible with those of the Treaty concerning the powers of the Court' and 'While being concerned that such interpretations should be such as to involve the least risk of provoking conflicts of jurisdiction, the possibility cannot be ruled out in advance that the judicial bodies concerned may arrive at different interpretations, which would have repercussions for judicial defendability'.[1]

---

[1] Paragraphs 18 *et seq.* Having issued this warning, the Court nevertheless accepted the validity of the procedure. It confined itself to expressing the view that the appointment of the 'Community' members of the Tribunal from among its own members was incompatible with the EEC Treaty.

It was because of concern over the same point that the EEC prevented the inclusion of arbitration clauses in the agreements concluded with the European Free Trade Association (EFTA) because they included provisions apparently so similar to those of the EEC Treaty that it would have been awkward if an *ad hoc* body had had to rule on the interpretation of those provisions and had arrived at conclusions differing from those of the Court of Justice on the subject.

Furthermore, as already noted, in the previously-mentioned *Polydor, Pabst* and *Kupferberg* cases, the Court in fact interpreted some provisions of those agreements.

This reserve is undoubtedly important. It is understandable that the Communities should seek to ensure that an outside body, unfamiliar with Community law, does not encroach even indirectly into the Community's 'internal affairs' by way of the interpretation of an agreement.

In law, however, the position of the Court of Justice in relation to an agreement is clearly similar to that of a State's national court's. Moreover, in the *Polydor* and other cases it was only by virtue of the applicability of these agreements to subjects of internal law that it was able to proceed to an interpretation, in the same way as internal courts.

On the other hand, the Court is clearly not entitled to judge on an 'international' procedure in which the Community is opposed to another contracting party.

It is, therefore, quite normal that there should be two bodies competent to interpret the agreement, one as regards international relations and the second as regards internal applicability.

B – Division of powers between the Commission and the Council for the purposes of settlement procedures

It has been noted that the introduction of an arbitration procedure or a procedure for settlement by a judicial body was liable to create problems as regards the division of powers between the Commission and the Council. There is no doubt of the need to decide which body is competent to appoint the arbitrators, to appoint officials and give them instructions.

Since there is no provision in the establishing Treaties and since, as already pointed out, neither of the two bodies has a monopoly as international representative of the Community, procedures would have to be laid down.

Clearly, however, this objection is of little consequence as compared with the importance and value of a procedure for settlement by arbitration.

C – Difficulties associated with 'mixed' agreements

At first sight, there are two possible solutions.

The first, which initially appears to be the simpler, would be to consider that the Community and the Member States form a single unit for the purposes of the settlement procedure, whatever the provisions of the agreement to which the dispute relates. The other contracting party would then be able to proceed against either the Community or the Member States. In all cases, the two would take the necessary decisions to initiate the procedure jointly and would act together.

It can be argued that this kind of procedure was implied by the provision in the Association Agreement with Greece stipulating that for 'the application of this procedure (arbitration) the Community and the Member States shall be deemed to be a single party to the dispute'.

The second solution, which is more complicated but much sounder in law, would be to consider that either the Community or one (or more) Member States are parties, and even to make it possible for the Community and one (or more) Member States to be sued jointly.

The problem was clearly understood and resolved in the Convention of 1 August 1976 for the protection of the Rhine against pollution by chemicals, which stipulates:

'In the event of a dispute between two contracting parties, one of which is a Member State of the EEC, the other party shall transmit its request to both the Member State and the Community, which shall jointly notify the party concerned within two months, whether the Member State or the Community, or the State and the Community together, are parties to the dispute. If such notification is not given in due time, the Member State and the Community shall be deemed to constitute one and the same party to the dispute for the application of this annex'.[1]

It also stems logically from the Convention on the Law of the Sea – on the basis of notification of the other parties of the division of powers between the Community and the Member States – that the dispute concerns sometimes the Community and sometimes a Member State.

Nevertheless, Article 7 of Annex IX provides – and therefore implicitly allows – that the organization and one or more Member States can make common cause.[2]

---

[1] Annex B/8.

[2] Article 7/3: 'When an international organization and one or more Member States make common cause, the organization is deemed to have accepted the same procedures for the settlement of disputes as those States. If one of those States has opted for the International Court of Justice only, in accordance with Article 287, the organization and that Member State shall be deemed to have accepted arbitration in accordance with the procedure laid down in Annex VII, unless the parties to the dispute agree to choose another method.'

It is conceivable that it may be necessary to make common cause in the event of a dispute involving both Community and State powers.

Such machinery is clearly not simple. In the particular case, however, the difficulty lies not with the settlement procedure as such but with the 'mixed' agreement itself which, as already noted, is a source of all sorts of complications.

To sum up, it is understandable that the Community should not systematically press for arbitration or similar procedures. It accepts them when they are a condition for negotiating an agreement. Its attitude in this respect is exactly the same as that of many States which consider that the inclusion of settlement clauses in an international agreement is a matter of expediency.

Conclusion

Our conclusions can be summarized as follows:

1. We have tried to describe the main problems created by the appearance of the European Communities as an 'actor' on the international stage. Relatively secondary questions, mainly of a technical nature, have been disregarded.[1]

2. Experience has made it possible to go into detail concerning some aspects of the situation of the European Communities in the international order; in the absence of significant 'precedents', other aspects remain uncertain.

   The facts presented on these subjects are therefore of a somewhat provisional character. On the other hand, its seems likely that short-term developments at least will be relatively limited in areas where there is a substantial amount of practice.

3. Overall, the position of the European Communities in the international order has reached a fair degree of maturity, as demonstrated, for example, by the acceptance of the EEC as a contracting party to a world-wide convention of such importance as the United Nations Convention on the Law of the Sea.

The situation should not, however, be regarded as fixed once and for all.

It has been noted that the solutions adopted for certain problems peculiar to the Communities have not always taken sufficient account of the requirements of their internal law. Reference has, *inter alia,* been made to the points where Community access to, and participation in, the work of international organizations and conferences should be improved and to the difficulties which can be created for the EEC by certain conditions laid down for its participation in multilateral conventions.

This being so, there is little doubt that, quite apart from the very special problem of their 'recognition' by the USSR and its allies, the Communities will still have to negotiate with their partners on many aspects of their international status.

---

[1] For example, when the deposit by the Communities of instruments accepting multilateral agreements, to which their Member States are also entitled to be parties, is not reckoned in calculating the minimum number of ratifications required for the agreements to enter into force (see, for example, Article 8 of Annex IX to the 1982 Convention on the Law of the Sea).

The outcome of these negotiations is very largely in the hands of the Member States of the Communities and will differ according to whether those States continue, as at present, to handle an essential part of their external relations individually, or whether they decide to take future international action through the Community.

Bibliography

In addition to the references in footnotes, a list is given below of a number of studies on the European Communities as a whole (including, therefore, their international powers) and of studies dealing specifically with the question of international powers and external relations.

ALTING VON GEUSAU, F.A.M., *The External Relations of the European Community*, Lexington, Mass., 1974.

BLECKMANN, A., *Europarecht, Das Recht der Europäischen Wirtschaftsgemeinschaft*, Heymanns, 1976.

BOULOUIS, J. and CHEVALLIER, R.M., *Grands arrêts de la Cour de justice des Communautés européennes*, Vols. 1 and 2, Paris.

BOURRINET, J. and TORELLI, M., *Les relations extérieures de la CEE, PUF, Que sais-je?*, Paris, 1980.

Colloque Liège 1964, *Les relations extérieures de la Communauté européenne unifiée*, Liège, 1969.

Colloque Nancy 1981, *L'Europe dans les relations internationales – Unité et Diversité*, Ed. Pedone, Paris, 1982.

Commission of the European Communities, *The European Community, international organizations and multilateral agreements*, Brussels, 1980.

Die Außenbeziehungen der Europäischen Gemeinschaft, wiss. Kolloquium, 4-5 April, Cologne s.d., 1975.

DINTILHAC, F., *L'applicabilité directe des dispositions des accords externes liant la CEE*, Mémoire DEA, Paris, 1 September 1983.

FLAESCH-MOUGIN, C., *Les accords externes de la CEE, essai d'une typologie*, Ed. University of Brussels, 1979.

FRANCK, C., *Option interne et externe pour la Communauté européenne, essai sur les finalités*, Centre d'études européennes, Louvain, 1975.

GANSHOF VAN DER MEERSCH, W., *Communautés européennes et droit international*, RCADI 1975, Sijthoff, 1978.

GROEBEN, H. (VON DER), BOECKH, TIESING, *Kommentar zum EWG-Vertrag*, Baden-Baden, 1974.

HELD, Ch. E., *Les accords internationaux conclus par la Communauté économique européenne*, Vevey, Switzerland, 1977.

HERMANN, R., *Das Abschlußverfahren völkerrechtlicher Verträge der EWG*, Berlin, 1973.

JACOT-GUILLARMOD, O., *Droit communautaire et droit international public,* Geneva, 1979.

JOZEAU-MARIGNÉ, Report to the European Parliament, Doc. 567/77, *La position de la Communauté en droit international public,* 8 March 1978.

KIM, C.O., *La CEE dans les relations commerciales internationales,* Institut d'études européennes, Université libre de Bruxelles, 1971.

KRUCK, H., *Völkerrechtliche Verträge im Recht der Europäischen Gemeinschaften,* Berlin, 1977.

LOUIS, J.V., BRUCKNER, P., *Le droit de la Communauté économique européenne,* Vol. 12, 'Relations extérieures'. Ed. of Université libre de Bruxelles, 1980.

MEGRET, J., 'La politique commerciale commune', in *Le droit des Communautés européennes,* Vol. 6, Politique économique, 1976.

MIGLIAZZA, A., *La Comunità europea in rapporto al diritto internazionale e al diritto degli Stati membri,* Milan 1964.

MONACO, R., *Lineamenti di diritto pubblico europeo,* Milan, 1979.

NAFILYAN, G., 'Le pouvoir de conclure des traités dans les Communautés européennes', Thesis, Paris, 1975.

O'KEEFE, D., SCHERMERS H.G. (joint work edited by), *Mixed Agreements,* Kluwer Deventer, 1983.

PESCATORE, P., *Les relations extérieures des Communautés,* RCADI 1961, Vol II.

PUISSOCHET, J.P., *L'élargissement des Communautés européennes,* Paris, 1974.

QUADRI, R. (and MONACO, TRABUCCHI, under the direction of), *Trattato istitutivo della Comunità economica europea,* Commentario, Milan, 1969.

RAUX, J., *Les relations extérieures de la CEE,* Ed. Cujas, Paris, 1966.

RAUX, J., 'Les accords externes de la CEE', Regular articles in the *Revue trimestrielle de droit européen,* Paris.

ROMOLI, A., *Les relations extérieures de la CEE, bilan et cohérence,* study by the ESC, Brussels, January 1982.

SIMON, D., GRILLO PASQUARELLI, E., KLEMAN, N., *La Communauté économique européenne dans les relations internationales,* Centre européen universitaire de Nancy, 1972.

SMIT, H., HERZOG, P., *The law of the European Economic Community. A commentary on the EEC Treaty,* Mathew Bender, New York.

Thirty years of Community law (joint study), the European Perspectives Series, Office for Official Publications of the European Communities, Luxembourg, 1983.

TIMMERMANS, W.A. VOLKER E.L.M., *Divisions of powers between the European Communities and their Member States in the field of external relations,* Kluwer, 1981.

TOMUSCHAT Chr., *Die gerichtliche Vorabentscheidung nach den Verträgen über die Europäischen Gemeinschaften,* Cologne, Berlin 1964.

TWITCHETT, *Europe and the World,* Europe Publications, London, 1976.

VAN DER MEERSCH (under the direction of), *Droit des Communautés européennes,* Les Novelles, Larcier, Brussels, 1967.

Various authors, *L'Association à la CEE, aspects juridiques,* Brussels, 1970.

WAELBROECK, M., *Traités internationaux et juridictions internes dans les pays du marché commun,* Brussels, Paris, 1965.

WELLENSTEIN, E., *25 years of European External Relations,* Office for Official Publications of the European Communities, Luxembourg, 1979.

WOHLFARTH (and EVERLING, GLAESNER, SPRUNG), *Die EWG. Kommentar zum Vertrag,* Berlin, Frankfurt, 1960.

Works published in English in the

european perspectives

Series

The European Community:
How it works

Emile NOËL

CB-28-79-390-EN-C

The finances of Europe

Daniel STRASSER

CB-30-80-980-EN-C

The Community legal order

Jean-Victor LOUIS

CB-28-79-407-EN-C

Thirty years of Community law

Various Authors

CB-32-81-681-EN-C

The Customs Union
of the European Economic Community

Nikolaus VAULONT

CB-30-80-205-EN-C

The European Monetary System

Origins, operation and outlook

Jacques van YPERSELE and Jean-Claude KOEUNE

CB-41-84-127-EN-C

Money, economic policy and Europe

Tommaso PADOA-SCHIOPPA

CB-40-84-286-EN-C

An ever closer Union

A critical analysis of the Draf Treaty
establishing the European Union

Roland BIEBER, Jean-Paul JACQUÉ
and Joseph H. H. WEILER

CB-43-85-345-EN-C

The rights of working women in the European Community

Eve C. LANDAU

CB-43-85-741-EN-C

The professions in the European Community

Towards freedom of movement and mutual recognition of qualifications

Jean-Pierre de CRAYENCOUR

CB-33-81-061-EN-C

The challenges ahead - A plan for Europe

Various Authors

CB-28-79-827-EN-C

The old World and the new technologies

Challenges to Europe in a hostile world

Michel GODET and Olivier RUYSSEN

CB-30-80-116-EN-C

In the same Series:

Combat pour l'Europe

La construction de la Communauté européenne de 1958 à 1966

Hans von der GROEBEN

CB-40-84-311-FR-C

Further details of these publications and of the various language versions available are to be found in the catalogue of the Office for Official Publications of the European Communities.

European Communities – Commission

The European Communities in the international order

By Jean Groux and Philippe Manin
Preface by President Gaston E. Thorn

Luxembourg: Office for Official Publications of the European Communities

1985 – 163 p. – 17.6 × 25.0 cm

The European Perspectives series

DA, DE, GR, EN, FR, IT, NL, ES, PT

ISBN 92-825-5137-7

Catalogue number: CB-40-84-206-EN-C

Price (excluding VAT) in Luxembourg
ECU 5.25   BFR 240   IRL 3.80   UKL 3   USD 4.50